INTERROGATING THE
FIRST TEN AMENDMENTS
THROUGH GAMES

SHALL MAKE, SHALL BE

THE BILL OF RIGHTS AT PLAY

EDITED BY
LAINE NOONEY
AND JOHN SHARP

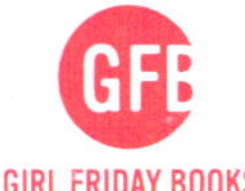

GIRL FRIDAY BOOKS

www.shallmakeshallbe.org

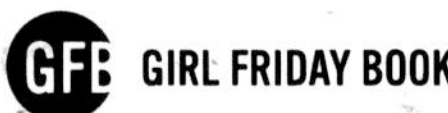

Published by Girl Friday Books™, Seattle
www.girlfridaybooks.com

Produced by Girl Friday Productions

Cover and interior design: Rachel Marek
Project management: Kristin Duran
Editorial production: Abi Pollokoff

Image credits: Paladin12/Shutterstock (paper texture): Cover, i–v, 1, 11, 21, 31, 39, 47, 55, 63, 73, 81; John Berens: vi, 2, 4–5, 6, 8–9, 10, 12, 14, 19, 20, 22, 28–29, 32, 35, 40, 45, 48, 56, 61, 62, 64, 70–71, 74, 80, 82, 85, 88–89; The STUDIO: viii–ix, x, 7, 25, 36, 52, 53, 54; Danielle Isadora Butler: xii, xiii, 66, 69, 72; Vi Trinh: xiv, 26, 27, 30; Andy Malone: 16, 17, 18; Latoya Peterson and Cherisse Santa Cruz Datu: 37; Shay Salehi: 38, 42, 43, 46; Shawn Pierre: 44; Peter Bradley: 51; Arnab Chakravarty, Ian McNeely, and Moaw!: 58, 59, 60; Ryan Kuo: 76, 77, 78, 79; arts.codes (Melissa F. Clarke and Margaret Schedel): 86, 87, 90

ISBN (hardcover): 979-8-218-00952-6
ISBN (ebook): 978-1-959411-22-2
Library of Congress Control Number: 2022910460

First edition

CONTENTS

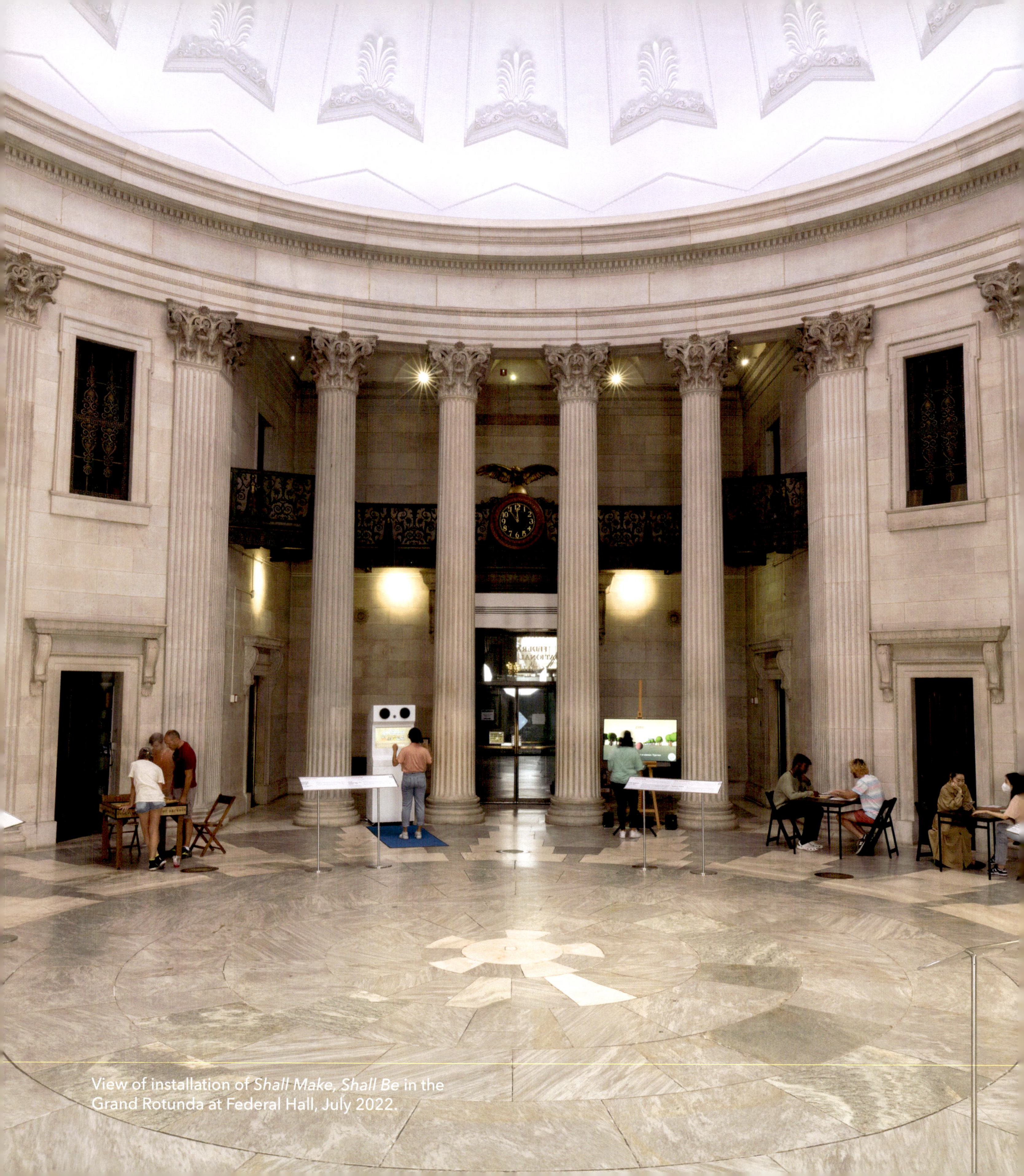

View of installation of *Shall Make, Shall Be* in the Grand Rotunda at Federal Hall, July 2022.

PREFACE AND ACKNOWLEDGMENTS

GOLAN LEVIN

Professor of Electronic Music, Carnegie Mellon University; Director and Codirector, Frank-Ratchye STUDIO for Creative Inquiry, 2009–2022

> We are proud to present this timely reflection on the rights that govern our lives, as refracted through the lens of the vital and popular medium of interactive games.

The Frank-Ratchye STUDIO for Creative Inquiry at Carnegie Mellon University supports atypical, antidisciplinary, and inter-institutional research at the intersections of the arts, science, technology, and culture. Since 1989, the STUDIO has served as a flexible laboratory for new modes of arts research, production, and presentation, providing opportunities for learning and dialogue that lead to the redefinition of the role of the arts in a quickly changing world.

It is in this spirit that the STUDIO is proud to support *Shall Make, Shall Be* as part of its mission. Simply put, the project is an exhibition of ten newly commissioned game artworks, each of which considers, in a bespoke and engrossing interactive format, the implications of one of the ten amendments to the US Constitution. These works have been developed by a diverse cohort of creators who work in the fields of playable art and critical game design. Their games are accompanied by essays, commissioned likewise from prominent legal scholars, which correspondingly consider timely social and ethical questions about each amendment. The *Shall Make, Shall Be* project—straddling contemporary art, game design, popular media, social activism, and constitutional law—is precisely the type of adventurous and interdisciplinary investigation that the STUDIO exists to foster.

This publication represents the capstone to a game-arts residency program conceived by our friend, frequent collaborator, and curator-in-residence R. Luke DuBois. We are proud to present this timely reflection on the rights that govern our lives, as refracted through the lens of the vital and popular medium of interactive games. The STUDIO expresses its gratitude to Luke for sharing with us the privilege of realizing this innovative, poignant, and ambitious program. We wish to thank our collaborative partners: editorial director Laine Nooney and curatorial and exhibition director John Sharp. We are also grateful to Luke, Laine, John, and the other members of our project's selection committee—Deborah Archer, Salome Asega, Shana Bryant, Jessica Hammer, Elizabeth Joh, Paolo

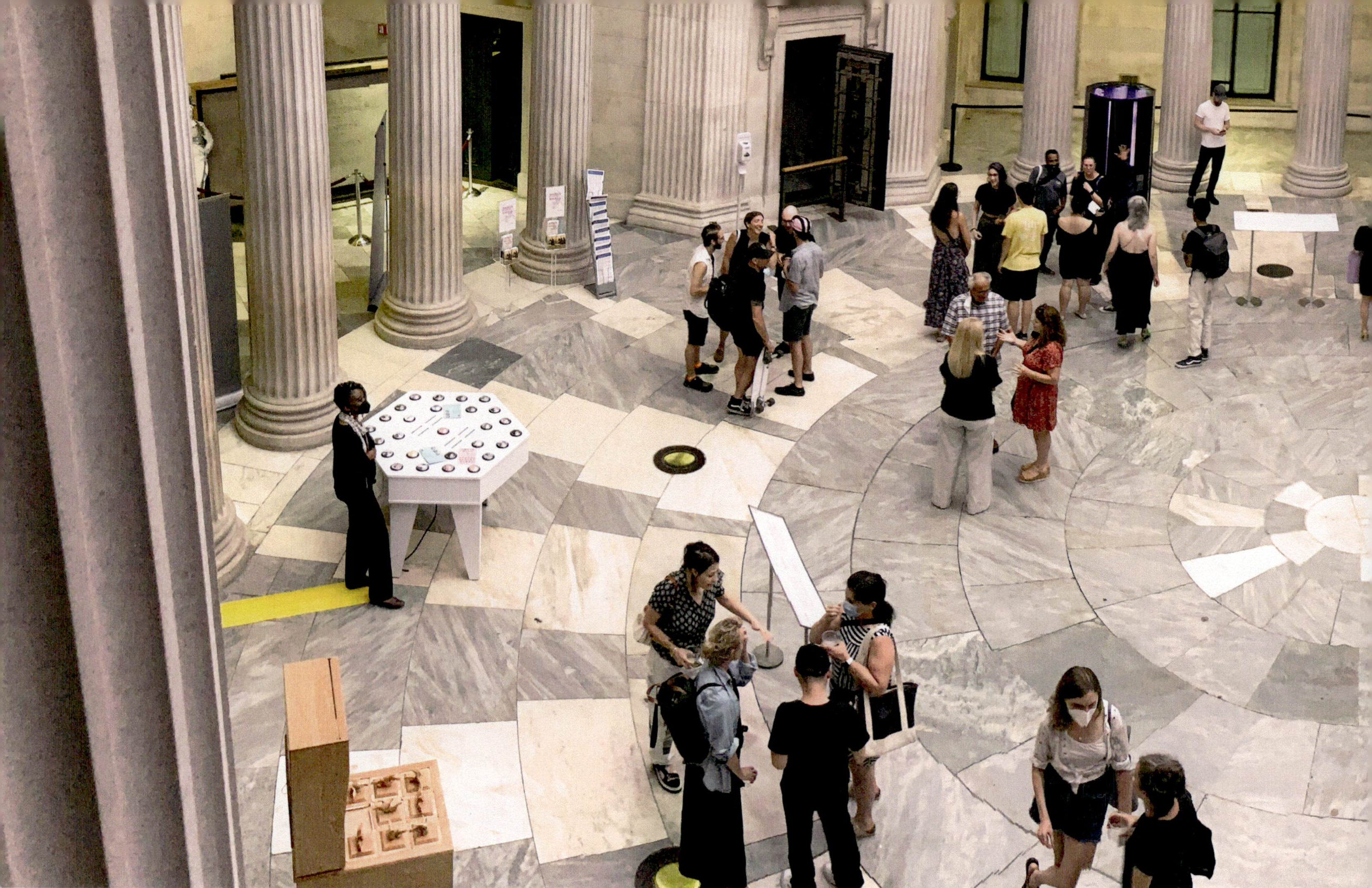

Pedercini, and Astria Suparak—who meticulously sifted through hundreds of applications to ensure that we commissioned a diverse, thoughtful, and capable cohort of artists. Their expertise in games, art, and law deeply enriched our team's own understanding of this project.

Many talented people have contributed their creative energy to the *Shall Make, Shall Be* project and its accompanying catalog. We are thrilled and proud to premiere the ten vibrant new works by the *Shall Make, Shall Be* commissioned artists—arts.codes (Melissa F. Clarke and Margaret Schedel); Peter Bradley; Danielle Isadora Butler; Ryan Kuo; Andy Malone; Arnab Chakravarty, Ian McNeely, and Moaw!; Latoya Peterson and Cherisse Santa Cruz Datu; Shawn Pierre; Vi Trinh; and Lexa Walsh—and we are grateful for the heart they have put into their creations. Likewise, we are indebted to Lea Rosen, Mike Wolfe, and Tim Hwang for advising the commissioned artists on constitutional law, and to the constitutional-law scholars who have gamely contributed essays to this unusual volume: Deborah Archer, Monica C. Bell, Jennifer Carlson, Erwin Chemerinsky, Jessica M. Eaglin, Keramet Reiter, Sharon E. Rush, Michael E. Shammas, Nabiha Syed, Suja A. Thomas, and Alexander Zhang. Their essays are essential and accessible guideposts to understanding the individual amendments in the Bill of Rights and the urgent social implications of the arguments that swirl around them in the early 2020s.

This production was realized through the effort of

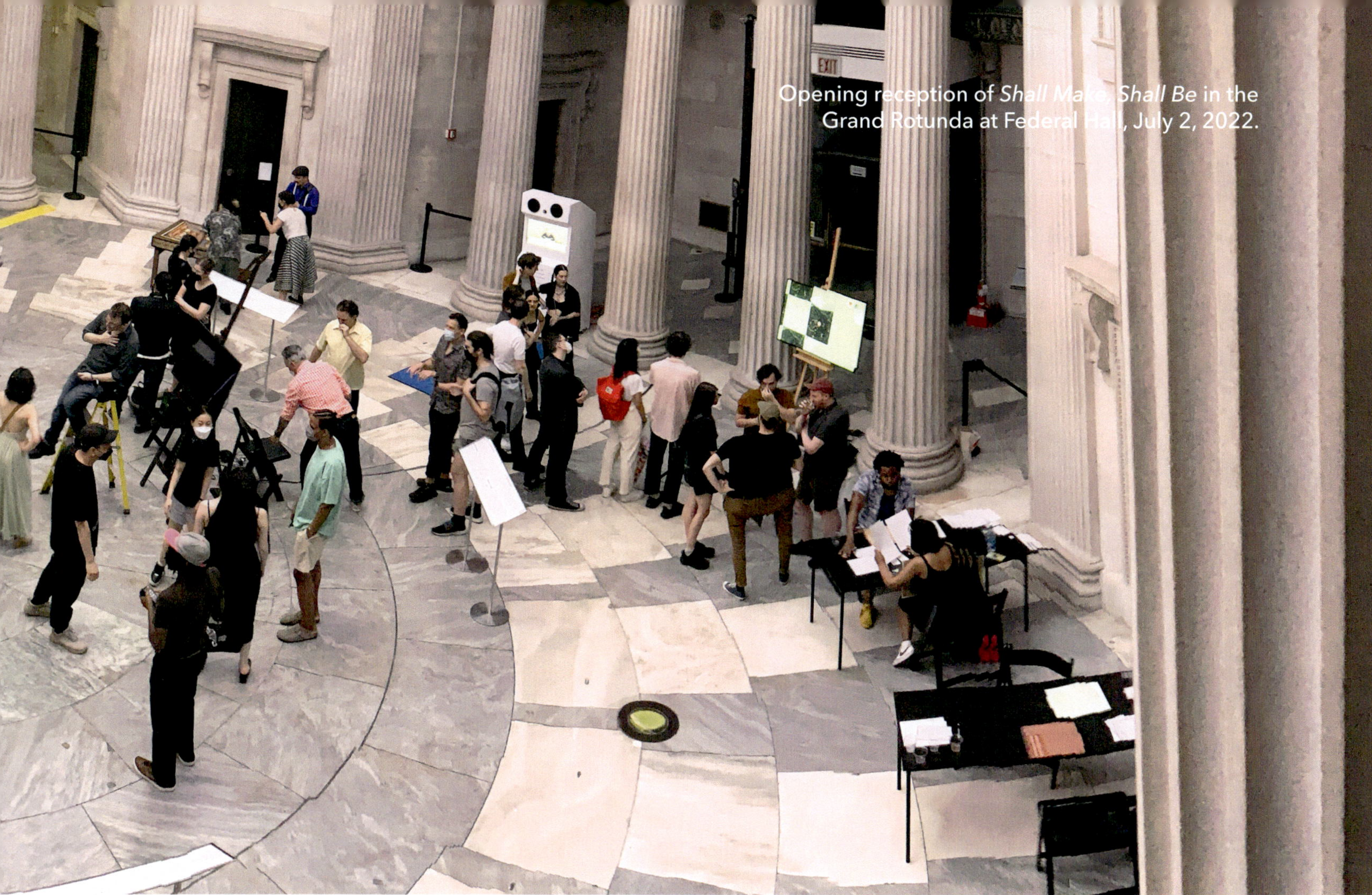

the STUDIO's tremendously dedicated staff, including former associate director Thomas Hughes, business administrator Linda Hager, financial assistant Carol Hernandez, and program coordinator Bill Rodgers. We are also indebted to the former dean of the CMU College of Fine Arts, Dan J. Martin, as well as advancement officers throughout Carnegie Mellon, for steering gifts and resources to the STUDIO that helped make this project possible: Carolyn Hess Abraham, Rebecca Abrams, Liz Cooper, Nancy Felix, Laura Herr, Denise Mieszkowski, and Daniella Staudacher.

We are humbled that the *Shall Make, Shall Be* exhibition debuted to the public at the Federal Hall National Memorial in New York City—the "birthplace of American government," where the Bill of Rights itself was enacted in 1789. We express our gratitude to Ellyn Toscano, Renee Barnes, and the Federal Hall staff for providing this singular and inspirational venue for the exhibition's premiere. We also thank our student research assistants, Ben Crystal and Shay Salehi, for their support in staging this exhibition.

The *Shall Make, Shall Be* project was made possible by a generous gift from David and Nathalie Cowan to the Director's Fund at the STUDIO for Creative Inquiry. We are immensely grateful to the Cowans for their faith, trust, and support, which has empowered us to realize not only *Shall Make, Shall Be* but also a wide swath of groundbreaking arts-research initiatives that cross boundaries, create new collaborations, push cultural norms, and advance the state of culture in our nation.

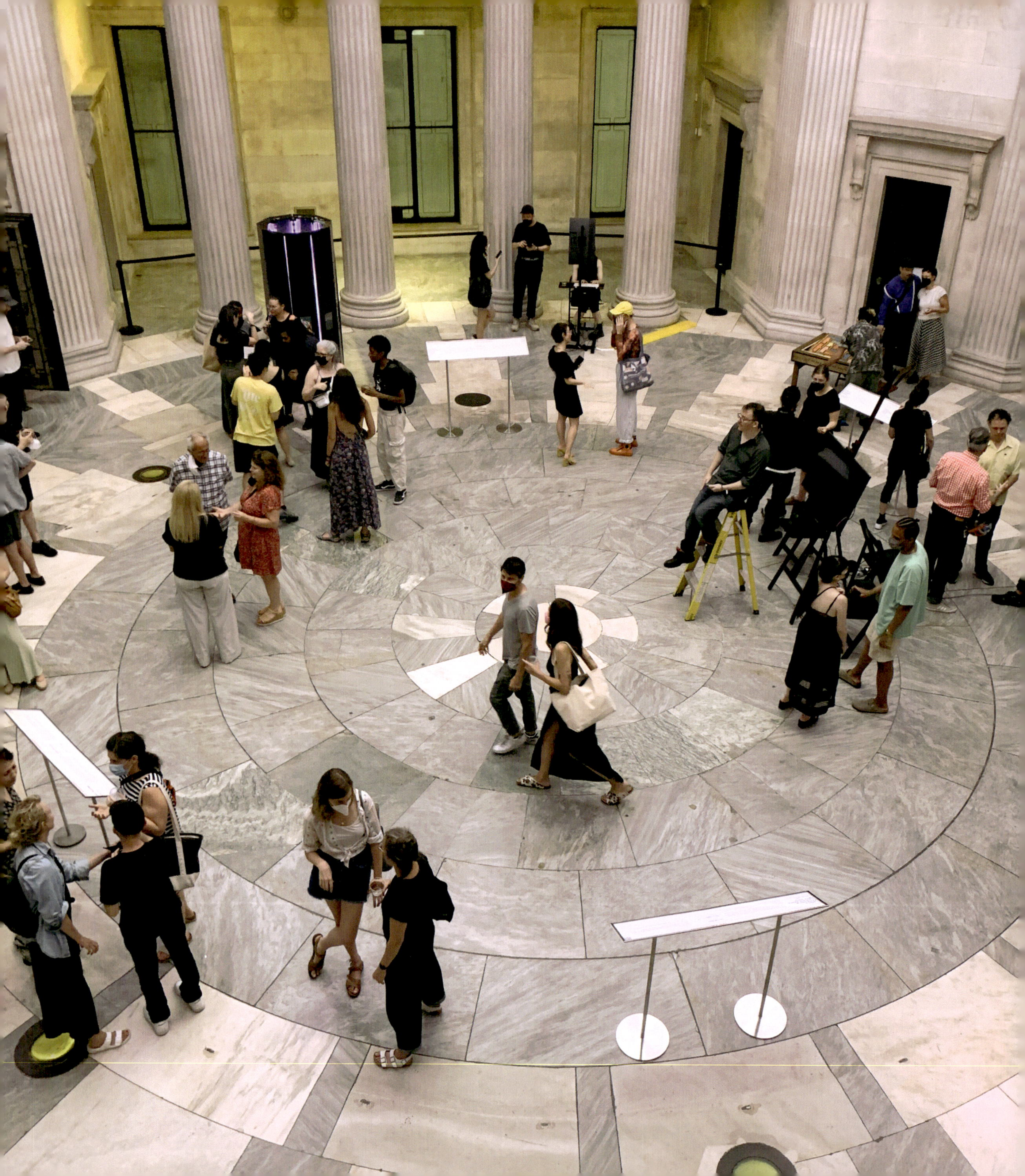

INTRODUCTION

R. LUKE DUBOIS New York University
LAINE NOONEY New York University
JOHN SHARP Parsons School of Design at The New School

> "Human rights may be guaranteed by law, but one's humanity is never a given."
>
> —Sarah Kendzior, *The View from Flyover Country: Dispatches from the Forgotten America*

The United States Bill of Rights (the first ten amendments to the US Constitution) is an integral part of American political and legal discourse and forms a core set of beliefs for the civil religion of the nation. The frequent citing of the Bill of Rights in casual conversation among Americans has no parallel in other countries; our understandings, misunderstandings, and varying interpretations of these rights and their implications are foundational to much of what unites and divides us as a nation. By reframing as rights those liberties that in the eighteenth century were available only to a privileged few, these ten amendments provide us with a Ten Commandments in reverse; rather than prescribing the behavior of the individual, they create explicit restrictions on what the higher power (in this case, the government) can do with regard to its citizens.

Today, our rights and responsibilities as citizens are being contested as never before. Evolving interpretations of the Constitution both reflect and perturb a rapidly changing world, impacting everything from the fabric and daily life of American society to our survival as individuals and even as a species.

Shall Make, Shall Be: The Bill of Rights at Play is a curatorial project that invited independent artists and game designers to create playable artworks themed around the individual amendments in the Bill of Rights, drawing on their effects, interpretations, and legal meanings in US culture. These works are meant to be understood as *critical games*, using the mechanisms of play to interrogate, critique, and inform our understanding of civil liberties in the twenty-first century.

Artists are obvious stakeholders in the First Amendment, alongside journalists, activists, and anyone else who sees the phrase "a more perfect union" as a call to action rather than a statement of fact. Our social discourse is openly political: we engage in satire, activism, participation, critique, and demagoguery, sometimes all in a single conversation. The ability for an individual in the United States to exercise their right to impugn the government is something that we frequently take for granted, and we easily forget that there are plenty of countries where this can get you fined, arrested, incarcerated, or killed. Most Americans, rightly, find such violence disturbing, but even more disturbing is the increasing number of Americans who don't seem to have a problem with it.

The Bill of Rights as a focal point certainly makes a lot of sense these days, given the frequency with which rights contained within come up in the lives of those in and around the United States. But games, play, and interactive artworks about the Bill of Rights? Not as obvious, perhaps, but definitely a timely way for reexamining and reconsidering the spectrum of rights articulated, interpreted, enacted, clung to, refuted, and otherwise swirling inside and giving structure to the American experiment. Indeed, games have overtaken the global film industry and also broken through to "serious" credibility as a mode of critical and contemporary art practice.

When we first proposed this project in the spring of 2016, the idea of commissioning *games* seemed like an accessible and educational medium for critically exploring the mechanics of the US Constitution: an interactive *Schoolhouse Rock!* for the twenty-first century. We hoped to highlight how games, which operate by proposing and enacting new modes of *direct participation*, can help us improve our cognitive model of the Bill of Rights. In the seven years since—following two presidential election cycles, three midterm elections, a Capitol insurrection, racial protests, and a global pandemic—our nation has become roiled in debate over what America is, whom it is for, what our country can require of us, and what we, as individuals, are allowed to

Exhibition view of Arnab Chakravarty, Ian McNeely, and Moaw!'s *Verbal Gymnastics* (white cabinet on left) and Peter Bradley's *Nomologos* (monitor on stand to right).

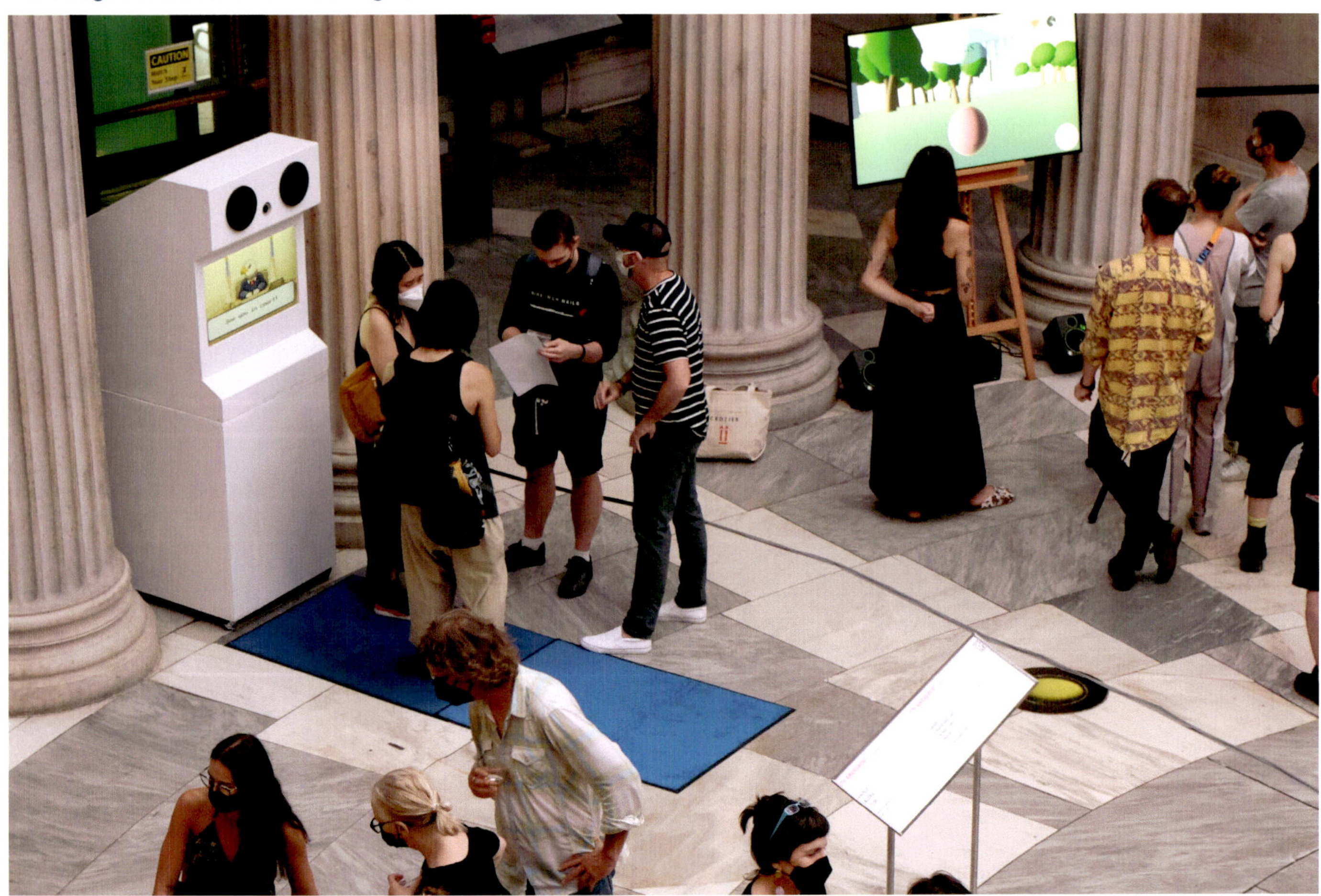

do. The Bill of Rights really is the napkin sketch for our understanding of what it is to be an American. Like all sketches, it leaves a lot of room for interpretation.

Shall Make, Shall Be provides ten interpretations through which we can play with these ideas. The games and interactive artworks in this exhibition come from clear points of view and open up lines of thinking about the meaning and implications of the framework we use to articulate the rights of citizens. One way to think of games is as playable systems. Not unlike life itself, gameplay shows us how our laws, cultural norms, and lived experiences don't always lead to the outcomes we may envision.

This has been our goal and hope for the *Shall Make, Shall Be* exhibition: to share ten works that give us a space to consider the underlying foundations of the American experiment and the identity and life these ten amendments created. In the pages that follow, you will find five elements for each amendment: the verbatim text of each amendment; an elucidating essay by a constitutional expert on the amendment's contemporary relevance; the artists' own thoughts on what concepts and principles inspired their project; documentation of the work itself; and our curators' notes on the work created about the amendment. We believe these works help us see new paths forward toward a chance at life, liberty, and the pursuit of happiness.

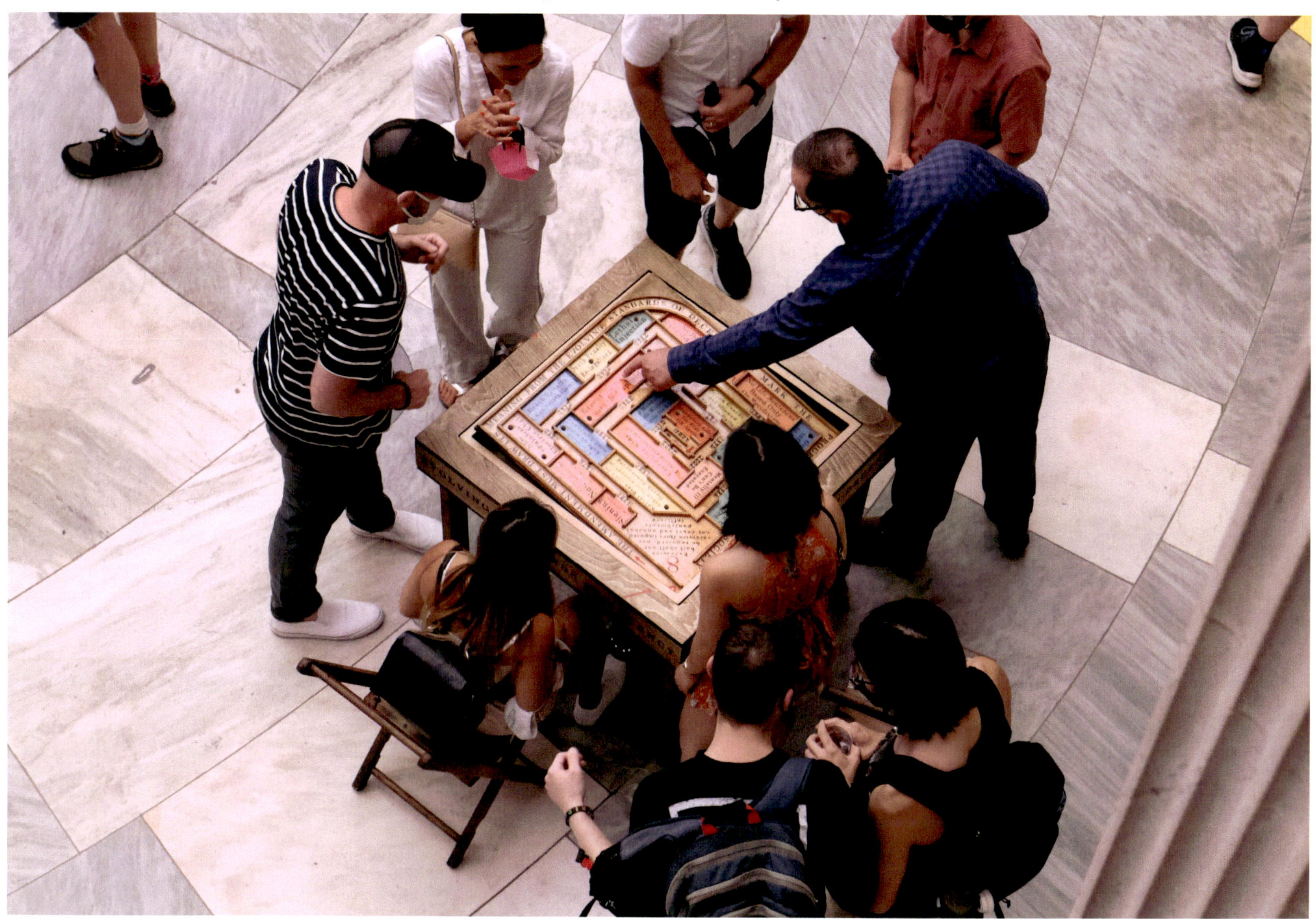

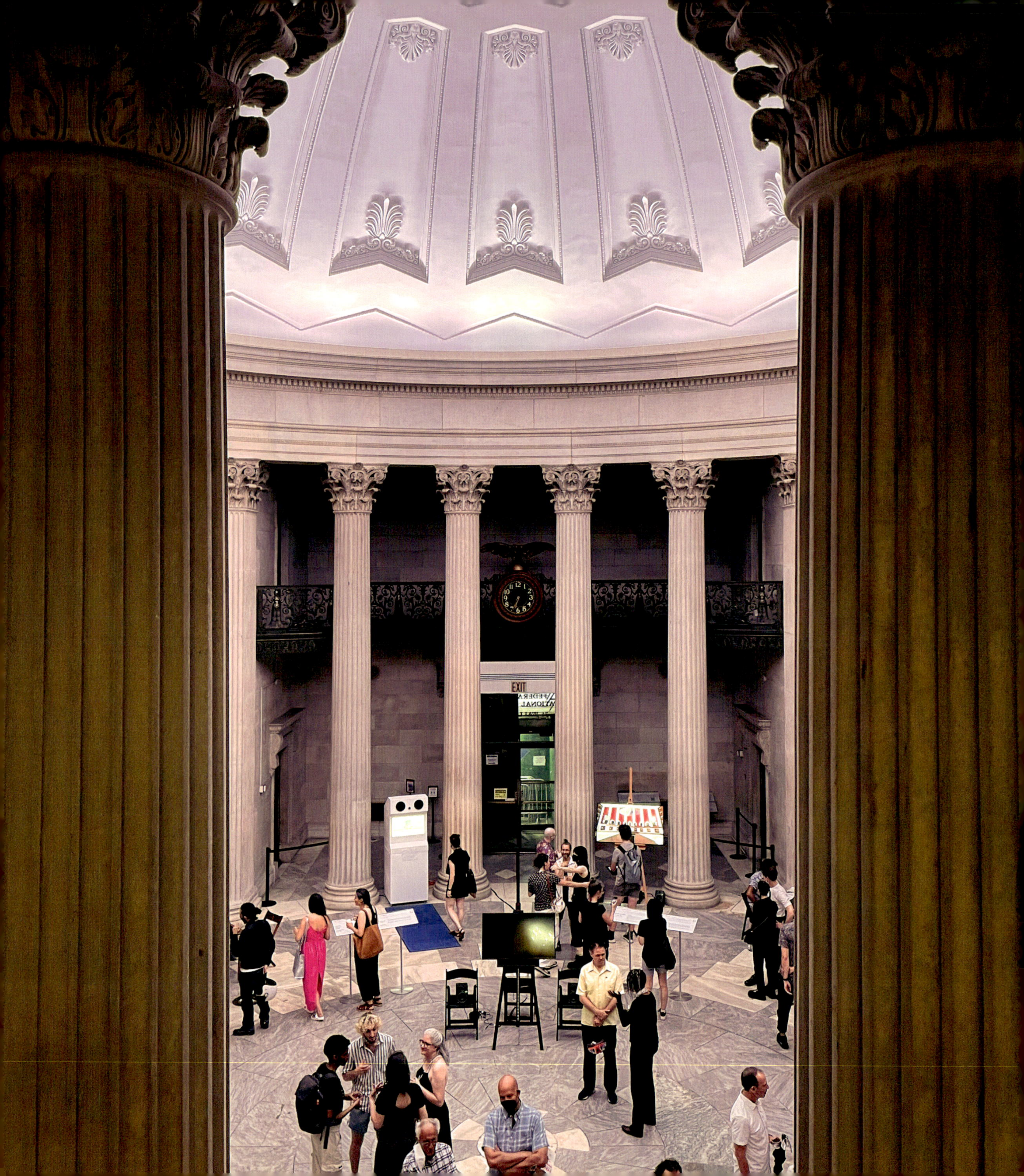

WHY THE BILL OF RIGHTS MATTERS

DEBORAH N. ARCHER

President of the American Civil Liberties Union;
Professor of Clinical Law, New York University

> One of the Constitution's critical shortcomings was its failure to name those fundamental rights that the new national government was bound to respect.

During the summer of 1787, delegates came together in Philadelphia to write the Constitution for the new United States of America. The Constitution is correctly considered a masterpiece of political organization and set the framework for what would become a beacon of democracy, liberty, and equality throughout the world. But that Constitution was also a deeply flawed document. It was born of compromise; it reflected the deep moral and political differences between the fifty-five white men in that room and the people they represented. The delegates debated the role and the future of slavery, the authority of the federal government, and the relative power of larger and smaller states in the federal government. Other questions that should have been foundational, such as the citizenship of Native Americans and women, were not even on the table.

One of the Constitution's critical shortcomings was its failure to name those fundamental rights that the new national government was bound to respect. The Federalists, advocates for a stronger national government, argued that a Bill of Rights was unnecessary.

Individual liberties were natural rights—*"We hold these truths to be self-evident, that all men are created equal, that they are endowed by their Creator with certain unalienable Rights, that among these are Life, Liberty and the pursuit of Happiness"*—and there was nothing in the Constitution that purported to take those rights away. Still, they argued, not unreasonably, it would be impossible to list all those rights and safer perhaps not to try. Furthermore, the genius of the separation of powers would ensure that competition among three coequal branches would prevent the federal government from usurping the rights of Americans.

The Anti-Federalists, supported by popular opinion, demanded an enumerated Bill of Rights. Having just fought for independence from a distant and imperious British government, many Americans were unwilling to risk trading one overweening power for another closer to home. As a result, in many states, ratification of the Constitution became contingent on the adoption of a Bill of Rights—an explicit statement of the federal government's inability to infringe on the rights of citizens.

The first ten amendments to the Constitution were

ratified by the states and adopted in 1791. They are written in the language of limited government—the amendments tell the federal government which laws it cannot adopt and which rights may not be infringed. The Bill of Rights does not claim to create those rights but only to preserve them against government interference. They also make clear that those rights listed in the Constitution are not exclusive.

Of course, the adoption of the Bill of Rights did not automatically create a more perfect union, nor did it ensure that all Americans could enjoy the freedoms described by the Declaration of Independence. Black people did not enjoy the security "in their persons, houses, papers, and effects" protected by the Fourth Amendment. Americans could not always rely on the right "peaceably to assemble" defended by the First. In a famous speech given sixty-one years after the Bill of Rights' adoption, Frederick Douglass would ask, "What to the Slave Is the Fourth of July?" One could ask that question about the Bill of Rights as well.

After the Civil War, the newly adopted Reconstruction amendments sought to bring Black people into the community of American citizenship. The amendments ended chattel slavery, asserted that Black people were citizens with the rights to due process and equal protection, and established that the right to vote "shall not be denied or abridged by the United States or by any State on account of race, color, or previous condition of servitude." Of course, the right to vote did not extend to Black women any more than it did to white women. Over time, the federal courts would use the Reconstruction amendments to extend the Bill of Rights' limitations on the federal government to state governments as well.

The Bill of Rights established a powerful and inspiring vision for America. In 1803, the United States Supreme Court in *Marbury v. Madison* established its ability to strike down acts of Congress that violate that vision, creating a pathway to make those rights real. But this power was rarely exercised. For over a century, the Courts rarely enforced the Bill of Rights.

And, of course, the Bill of Rights, even as extended by the Reconstruction amendments, has never in fact fully and effectively defended the natural rights of all Americans. After centuries of struggle, America continues to resist giving life to its lofty founding principles. Racial oppression remains an essential element of American law and society. Women, immigrants, the LGBTQ community, Native Americans, Latinx, Asian Americans, religious minorities, and other disfavored groups continue to face opposition as they seek to enjoy those freedoms that the founders viewed as so fundamental to life in the new democracy.

Much has been said and written about America's "racial reckoning" after the murder of George Floyd in May 2020. We see in Mr. Floyd's story, and in the popular uprising that followed it, the story of the Bill of Rights in all its glory and limitations. Where were the Fourth, Fifth, and Eighth Amendments when Mr. Floyd was murdered by police in front of a crowd in broad daylight? Where was the First Amendment when protesters were systematically harassed, beaten, and arrested in communities around the country?

The story of America remains, in so many ways, the story of a country that is still striving to live up to the words that framed its birth, the story of a country that is working to honor the sacrifices of the countless Americans who have given their lives to give those words meaning. The Bill of Rights matters today because America matters today. Our nation faces an existential crisis as those who believe in democracy struggle against those who seem to favor rule by strongman. The result of that struggle will matter not only for Americans but also for those around the world who gain inspiration from our story as they fight against totalitarianism and oppression.

THE FIRST AMENDMENT

Congress shall make no law respecting an establishment of religion, or prohibiting the free exercise thereof; or abridging the freedom of speech, or of the press; or the right of the people peaceably to assemble, and to petition the Government for a re-dress of grievances.

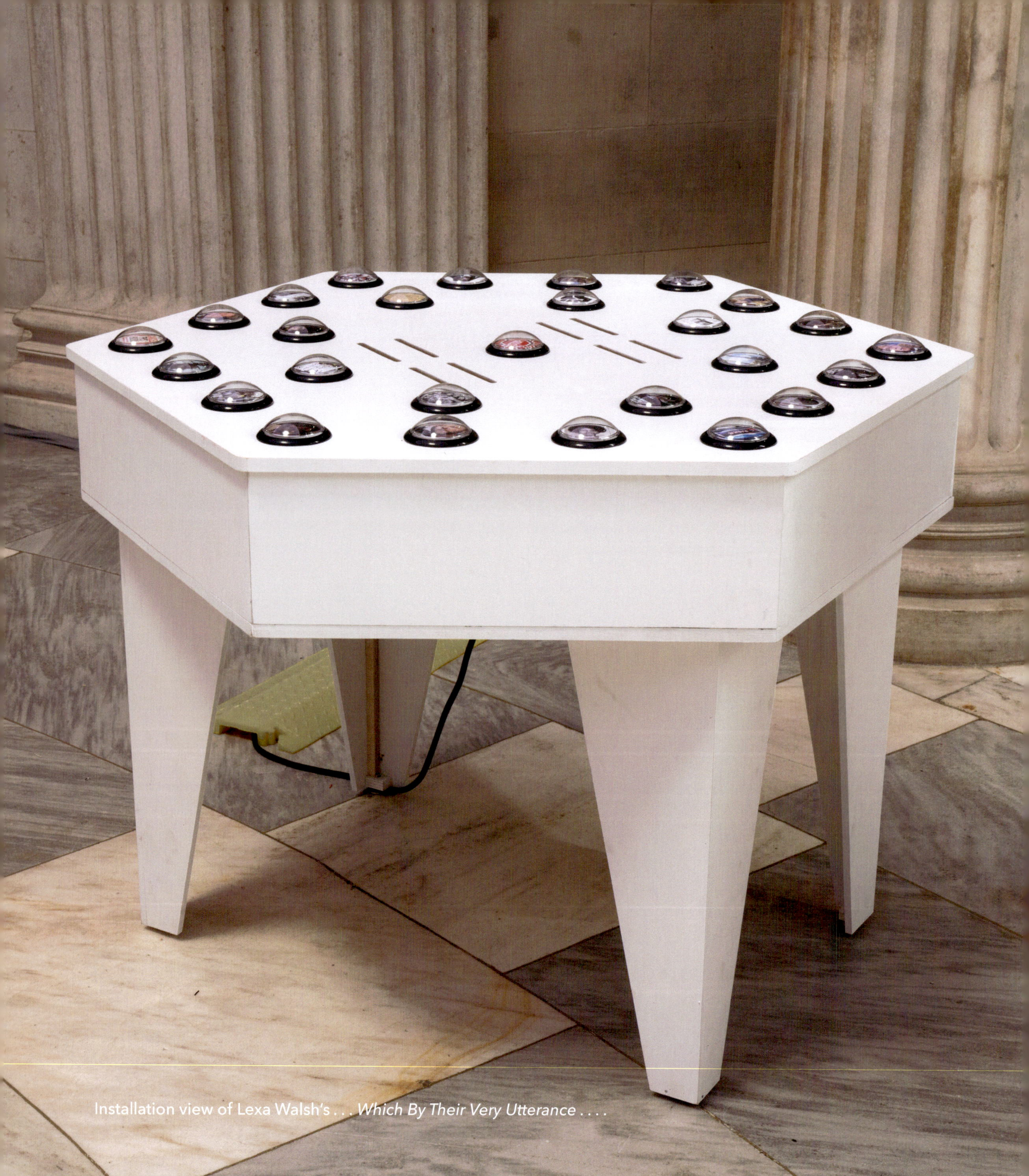

Installation view of Lexa Walsh's . . . *Which By Their Very Utterance* . . . .

Lexa Walsh
. . . *Which By Their Very Utterance* . . . , 2022
Wooden game board, electronics,
    computer, sound, website, printed matter
47 inches by 54 inches by 42 inches

Observing ugly truths about our world is a necessary step toward improving them.

INTERROGATING THE FIRST AMENDMENT

NABIHA SYED

CEO, The Markup

Much of modern First Amendment conversation is about limits: When does free speech become harassment? When does a gathering become a riot, outside the bounds of legal protection? When do opinions become incitement to violence? But while we spend much energy on what we can *say*, we devote surprisingly scant attention to how those sayings are formed—that is, what we can *know*, and how the First Amendment plays a part.

Take, for example, the unforgettable worldwide protests around racial justice in 2020. Demonstrations followed the horrifying killing of George Floyd in Minneapolis, Minnesota, documented in a cell phone video taken by seventeen-year-old digital activist and filmmaker Darnella Frazier. Her instinct to document the violence unfolding in front of her was commendable and made possible by handheld technology. Should the First Amendment protect this kind of fact-finding?

It should—but it doesn't in many jurisdictions, including the federal circuit that encompasses Minnesota. Thankfully, other federal circuits have begun to recognize the right to record the police, as Ms. Frazier bravely did, as protected by the First Amendment. But this is only a recent turn. Recognized in 2012 in the Illinois case *ACLU v. Alvarez*, the right to record is considered part of more commonly embraced rights: "The act of making an audio or audiovisual recording is necessarily included within the First Amendment's guarantee of speech and press rights . . . The right to publish or broadcast would be insecure, or largely ineffective, if the antecedent act of making the recording is wholly unprotected."

The *Alvarez* logic builds on something foundational to our democracy. As the Supreme Court reasoned in a slightly older but landmark First Amendment case, *Richmond Newspapers v. Virginia* (1980), "[p]eople in an open society do not demand infallibility from their institutions, but it is difficult for them to accept what they

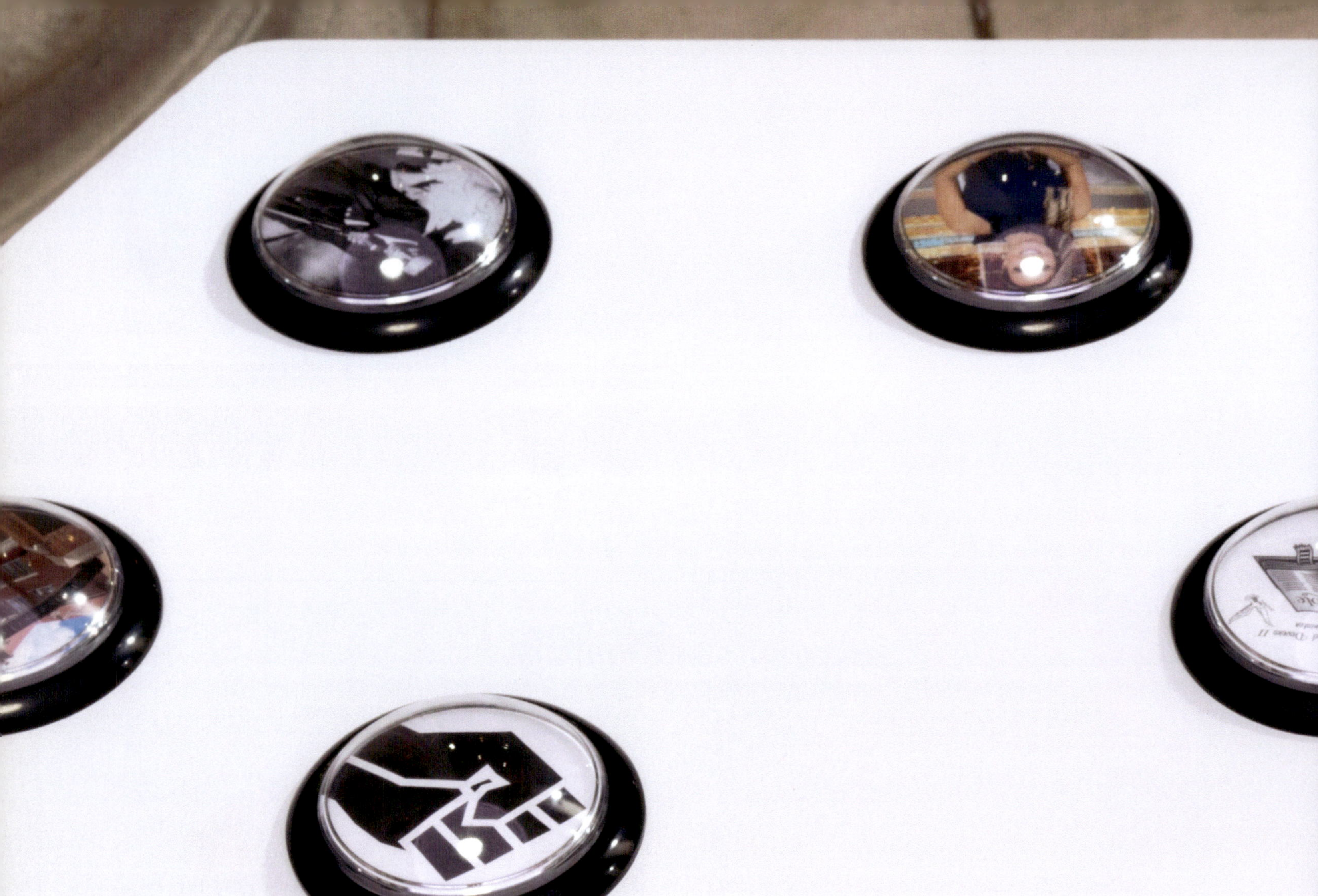

are prohibited from observing." This case went on to establish an affirmative First Amendment right—called "the right of access"—to observe and to obtain information about governmental proceedings.

This logic is important. Observing ugly truths about our world is a necessary step toward improving them. In our legal imagination, that change happens through our speech, our protest, and our petitions to the government—that is, our core First Amendment rights that allow us to self-govern and to agitate for change when needed.

But while American courts have finally recognized the theory, much work is needed in practice. The right of access has had uneven success when applied to court proceedings in Guantánamo Bay, Cuba, or even civil court dockets. A host of court-like administrative proceedings—including police disciplinary hearings and deportation proceedings—still lie outside the realm of the First Amendment right of access—and therefore outside the realm of true public oversight. With these systems of power cloaked in secrecy, how can we understand whether justice is properly served? Where do we get the facts that we need to organize?

The dramatic rise of private power only exacerbates the information asymmetry. Take, for example, the rise of "ag-gag" laws over the last decade, lobbied for by

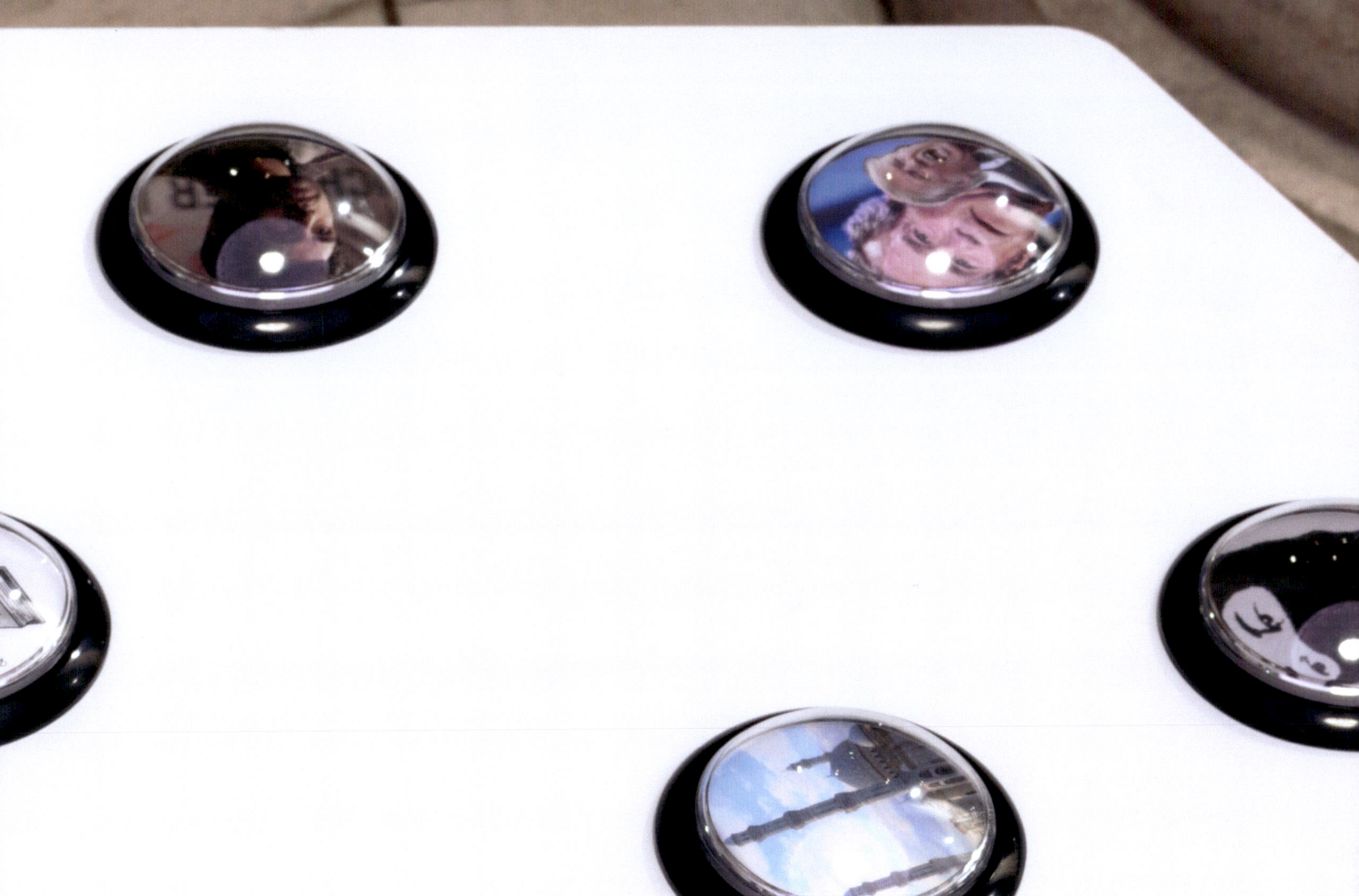

corporations that want to criminalize undercover investigations that reveal abuses on farms. While courts are striking down these laws, often after expensive and protracted litigation, the chilling effect on reporting and activism is real. Tech companies like Facebook similarly try to dissuade researchers and reporters from evaluating bias and discrimination on their platforms, arguing that data-collection efforts should fall under a federal antihacking law. This threatens the work of investigative reporters focusing on Big Tech, like my colleagues at the Markup; we have filed a brief in the Supreme Court arguing for First Amendment protections for our journalism.

Until we protect our quest for facts as fully as we protect our right to speak about them, our discourse will be impoverished. The power of a video, of data, of hard facts, is undeniable.

We should understand the First Amendment right of access—really, the right to understand and collect information about the reality of our world, no matter what powerful actors may say to the contrary—as a predicate, foundational right that gives meaning to other First Amendment rights of speech, assembly, press, and petition. The next frontier of the First Amendment struggle is to defend our right to know, not only our right to express.

. . . Which By Their Very Utterance . . . is a physical, interactive audio experience for one or more players. Each button, when pressed, plays an audio clip related to freedom of speech. The inner circle of buttons offers long playing and polyphonic loops, while the outer circle provides short samples. The center button stops a loop. There are no explicit win conditions and players should combine freely!

The First Amendment has a rich history of being exercised in sound: the freedoms of speech, religion, press, assembly, and protest reverberate in song and spoken language. . . . *Which By Their Very Utterance . . .* is a playable game/musical instrument/sound station that explores ideas embedded in the First Amendment. These ideas take shape in audio samples from educational videos, religious and spiritual practices, newsrooms, speeches, and marches, from Black Lives Matter protests to Stop the Steal rallies. I've selected samples referencing First Amendment court cases, such as those popularly known as "Scabby the Rat," regarding the twelve-foot-tall inflatable rat called Scabby that has been used as a symbol in union

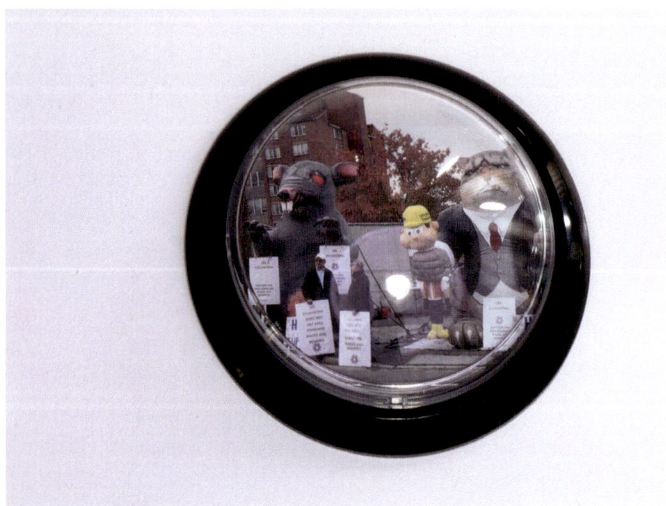

disputes, and "the Cursing Cheerleader," regarding the high school student whose social media post got her kicked off the junior varsity squad, as well as a few musical interludes (where I am practicing "fair use"). Visitors can exercise their own freedom of expression by playing the work. As they weave contemporary and historic sounds, they are emboldened to explore our First Amendment rights and to reflect on and interrogate their contents. An accompanying zine and website (www.utterance.space) allow users to dig more deeply into these sounds.

This work invites courageous dialogue, curiosity, and fun. It also aims to promote equity, not only by inviting users' participation and creativity but also through its varied content, to create new narratives that become ripe conversation starters. What do we uncover, for instance, when we juxtapose sounds from multiple religious practices, or play protests from opposing ideologies in tandem? I am particularly interested in the weaponization of cancel culture, a right-wing tactic that has been reclaimed by the left, often to its own detriment. Though it can be an effective tool for activism, it can also shut down meaningful exchange, reflecting the punitive culture and oppression many wish to overcome.

I've included clips from Fox News along with clips of progressive critic Dan Kovalik and other samples. We need to live in a society that ensures the right to open communication and the practice of it. Simply having these rights does not mean we know how best to wield them. Therefore, I've provided tips on active listening in the accompanying zine. With the freedom guaranteed by the First Amendment comes great responsibility.

Special thanks to Leo Knapp for technical assistance.

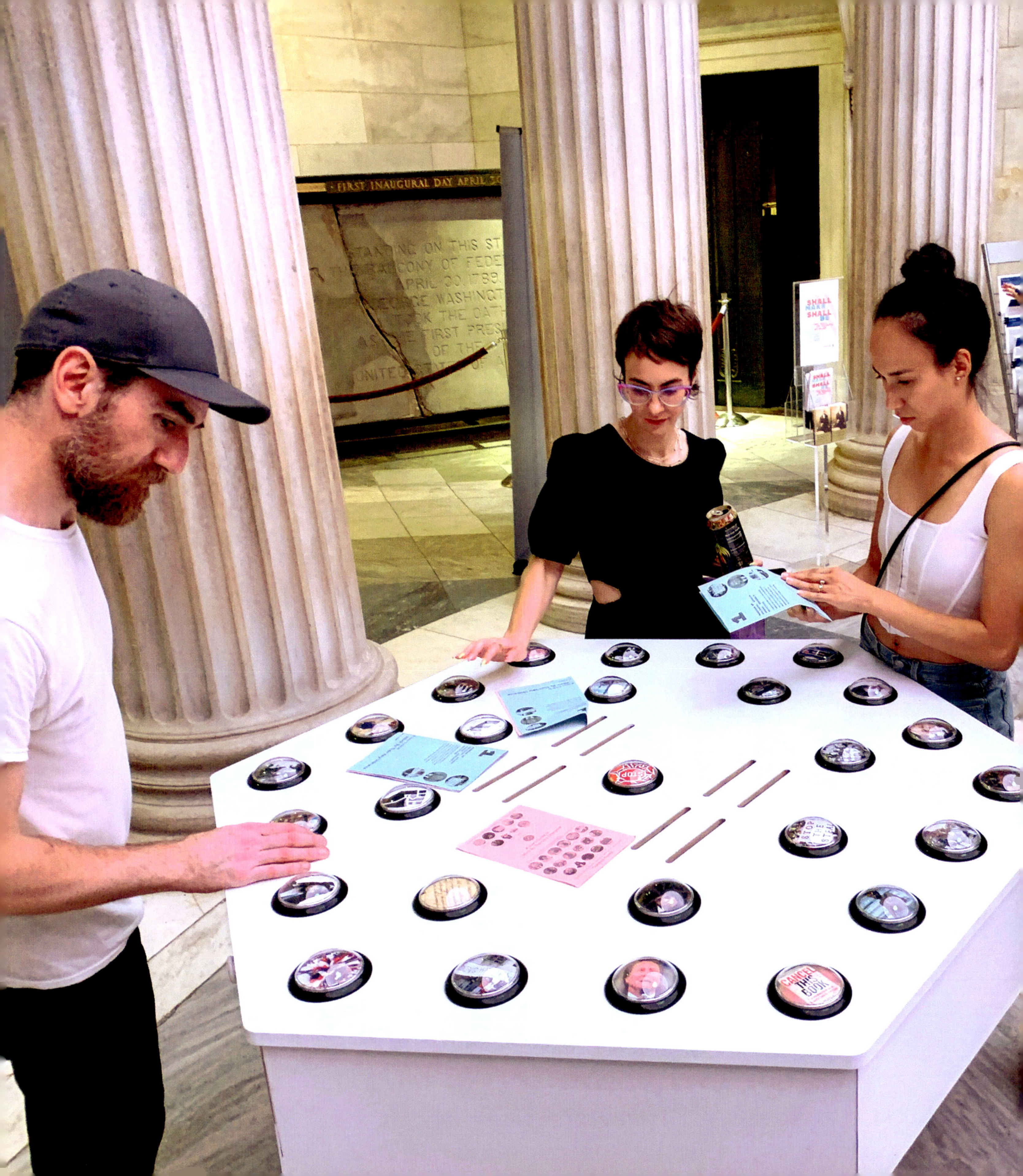

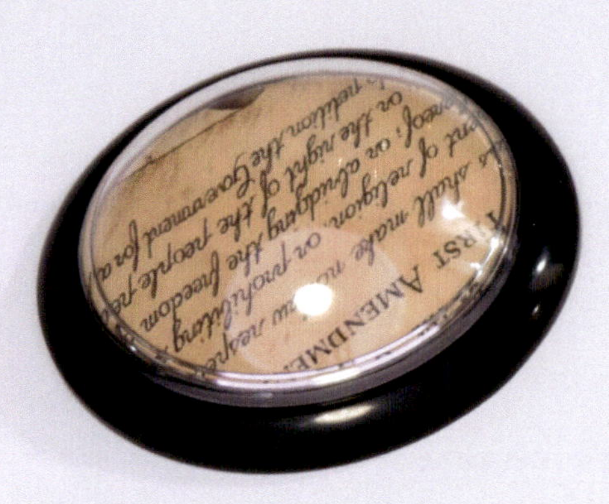
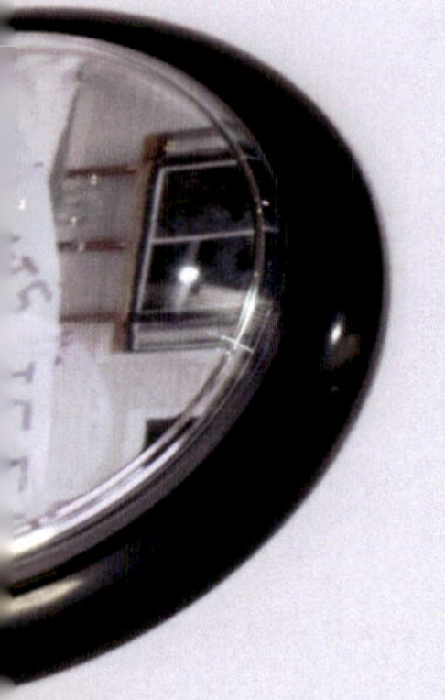
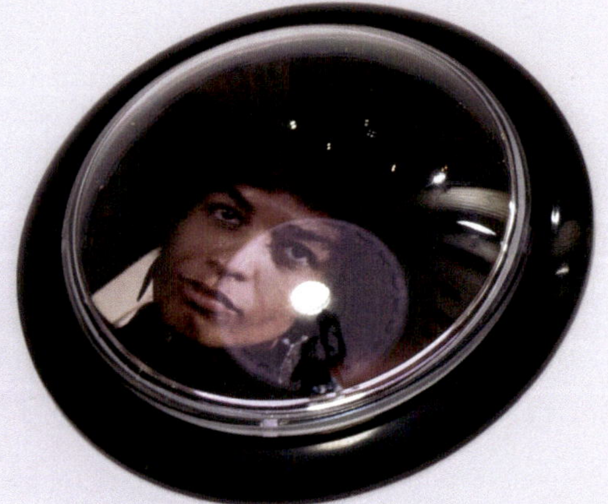
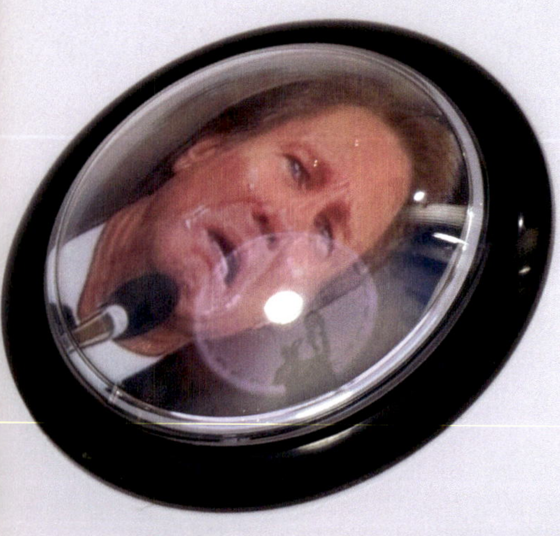

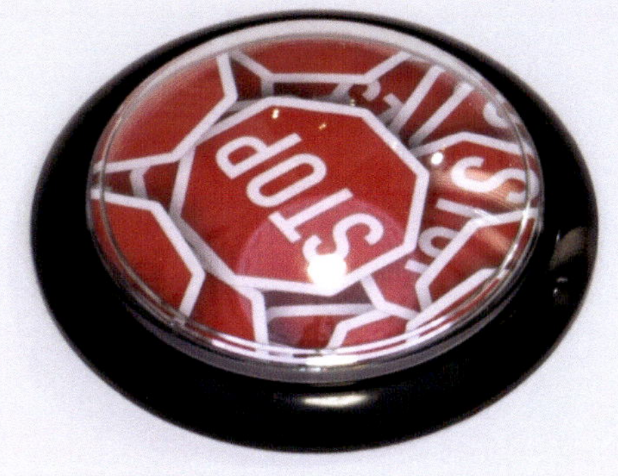

STOP

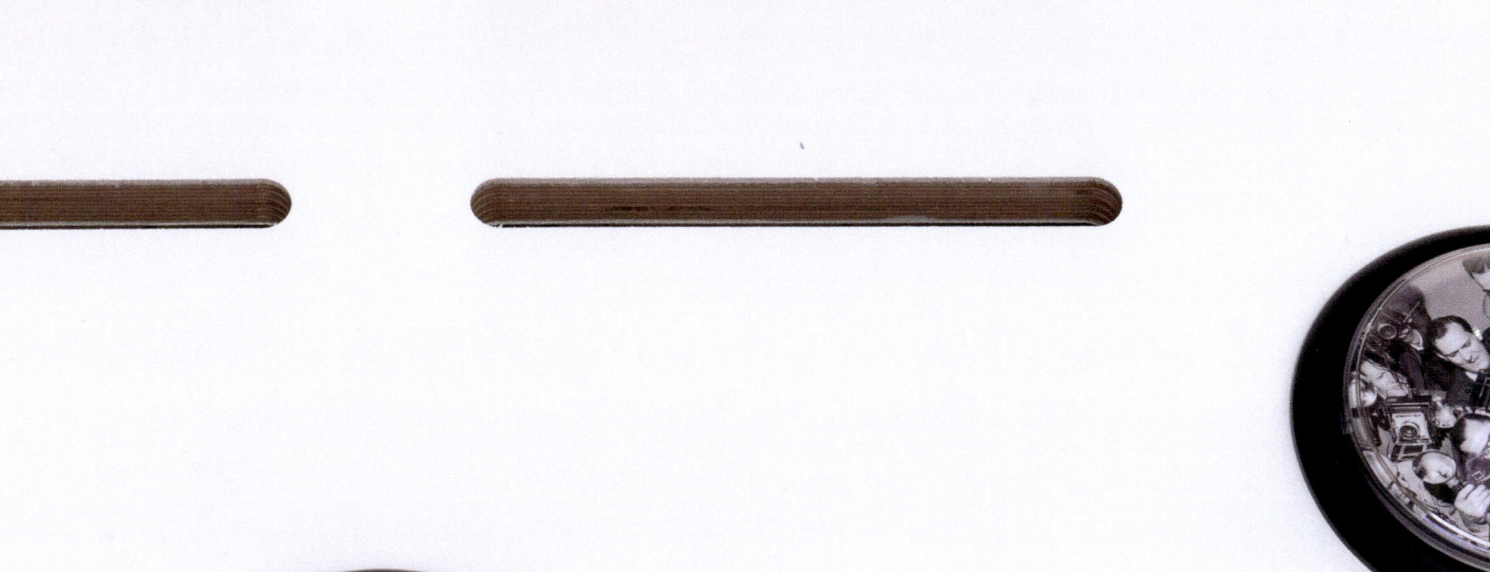

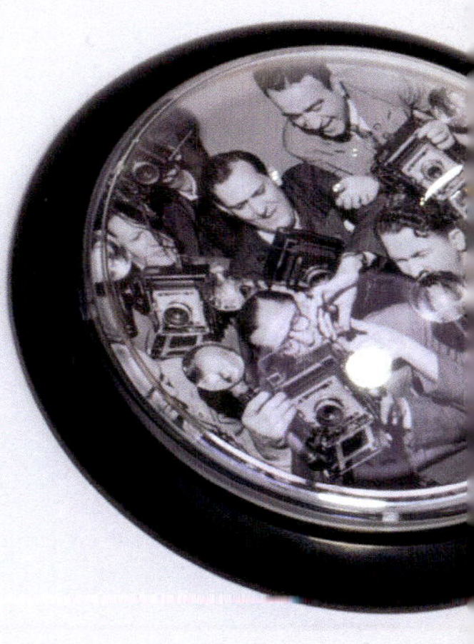

STOP
THE
STEAL

The First Amendment is a paradox. We retain the right to be heard, but not understood; we retain the right to speak, but also the right to misspeak; we retain the right to report, though not necessarily the truth. The amendment does not—and really, could it?—provide mechanisms to ensure comprehension, to parse truth from fiction, to authenticate. Indeed, the gulf between expression and knowledge is vast.

Somewhere between a musical instrument and a game of whack-a-mole, Lexa Walsh's . . . *Which By Their Very Utterance* . . . lays these paradoxes bare and exposes the gap between the protection of one's right to express and the ripples created by that expression. Walsh's work treats all utterances as equally valid: protests against police brutality against Black people are on the same ground as cries of support for election falsehoods, recordings from court cases with oppositional outcomes, excerpts from cultural practices ranging from education to music to religion. The presumed neutrality of the audio tracks belies the inequities in the First Amendment—if everything is of equal standing, how can we reasonably find meaning in the cacophony?

Walsh's work invites us to play these recordings by pressing large buttons. The more buttons the player presses, the more recordings play back, leading to a barrage of First Amendment–supported utterances. How we receive, interpret, and act upon these sounds is totally up to the player and their spectators. Not unlike the First Amendment, the work does not suggest why you might want to do this; it only presents you with the opportunity. Do you choose to engage playfully in order to have a little fun? Aesthetically, as if performing with a musical instrument? Methodically, so as to carefully consider each excerpt? With the spirit of a spoilsport to create chaos? Polemically, to draw attention to a particular utterance and its point of view? . . . *Which By Their Very Utterance* . . . distills the First Amendment to its essence, leaving us to find purpose and meaning not only in what we say but also in how we receive that uttered by others.

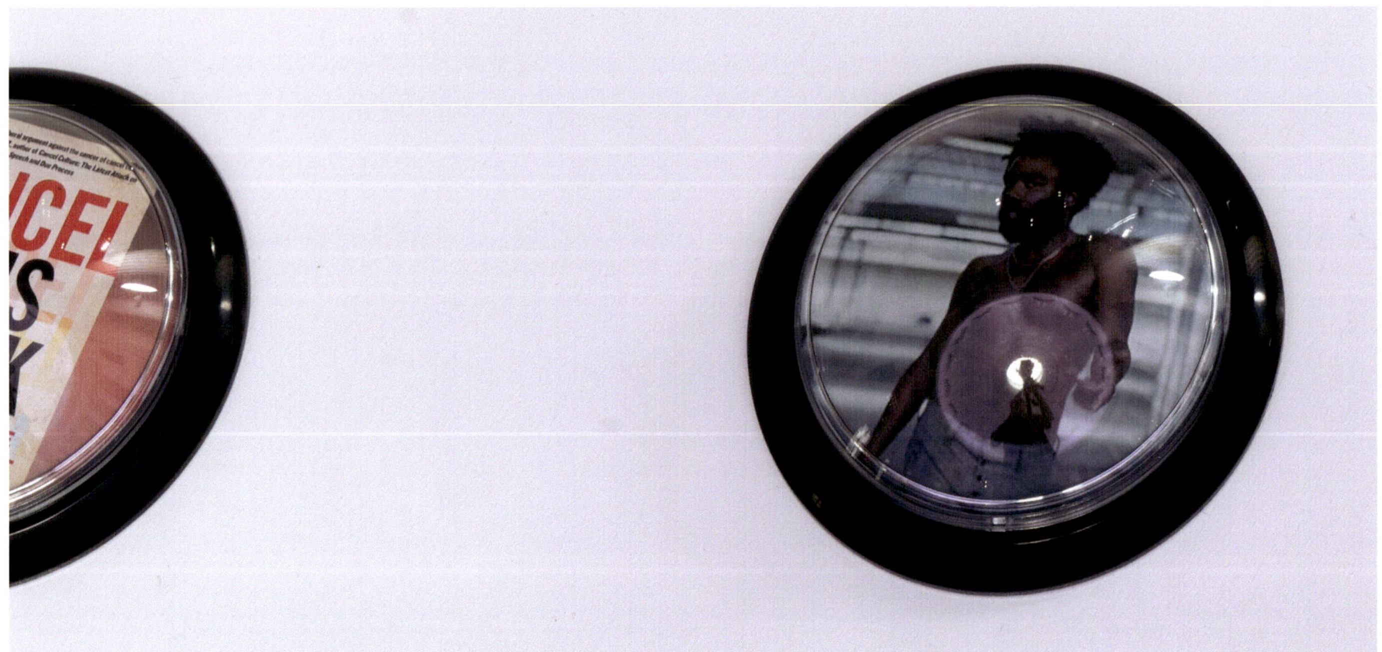

THE SECOND AMENDMENT

A well regulated Militia, being necessary to the security of a free State, the right of the people to keep and bear Arms, shall not be infringed.

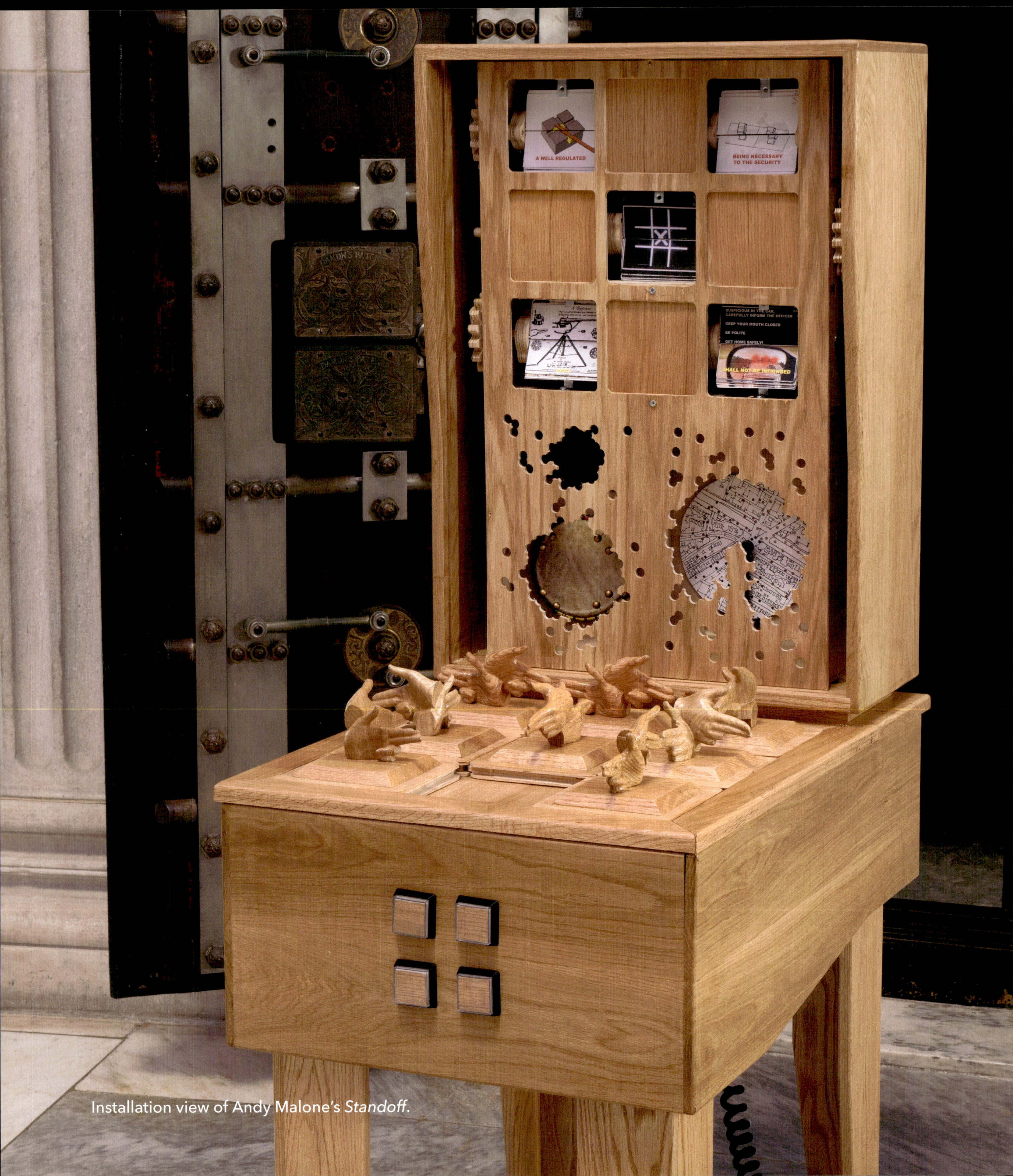

Installation view of Andy Malone's *Standoff*.

Andy Malone
Standoff, 2022
Wooden puzzle with mechanisms
23 inches by 31 inches by 66 inches

INTERROGATING THE SECOND AMENDMENT

The twenty-seven words of the Second Amendment enshrine one of the most controversial and consequential constitutional rights.

JENNIFER CARLSON
Associate Professor of Sociology and
Government & Public Policy, University of Arizona

Ratified in 1791, the Second Amendment has since become a battleground for public-health scholars looking to interrupt gun violence, firearms enthusiasts looking to protect gun rights, political pundits on the forefront of the so-called culture wars, and legal scholars and historians looking to parse out its meaning. Some thought it an anachronism, as outdated as the institution of the militia it referenced. Others believed that it provided a protective salve against all gun restrictions. By the dawn of the twenty-first century, many hoped that the US Supreme Court would settle the truth of the Second Amendment once and for all, and in the 2008 *District of Columbia v. Heller* case, it tried to do exactly that. In a 5–4 decision, the Court held that owning a handgun is an individual right protected by the US Constitution.

The *Heller* decision presented a complicated history of guns in American society as a redemptive tale of individual rights. But even within the *Heller* decision—with its troublingly brief references to "invasion" and "insurrection"—is recognition that guns did more than just ward off British tyranny in the eighteenth and nineteenth centuries. As historian Roxanne Dunbar-Ortiz argues, guns helped build the early American state as a white-settler republic through the ruthless extermination of Indigenous peoples in pursuit of their lands and the violent enslavement of African peoples in expropriation of their labor.[1]

Following the Civil War, guns served as tools of terror as whites in the South and beyond engaged in violent lynching campaigns and populated the ranks of white-supremacist terrorist groups like the Ku Klux Klan. As Northerners retreated from the South at the nineteenth century's close to wage war against Indigenous peoples in

---

1. Roxanne Dunbar-Ortiz, *Loaded: A Disarming History of the Second Amendment* (San Francisco: City Lights Books, 2018).

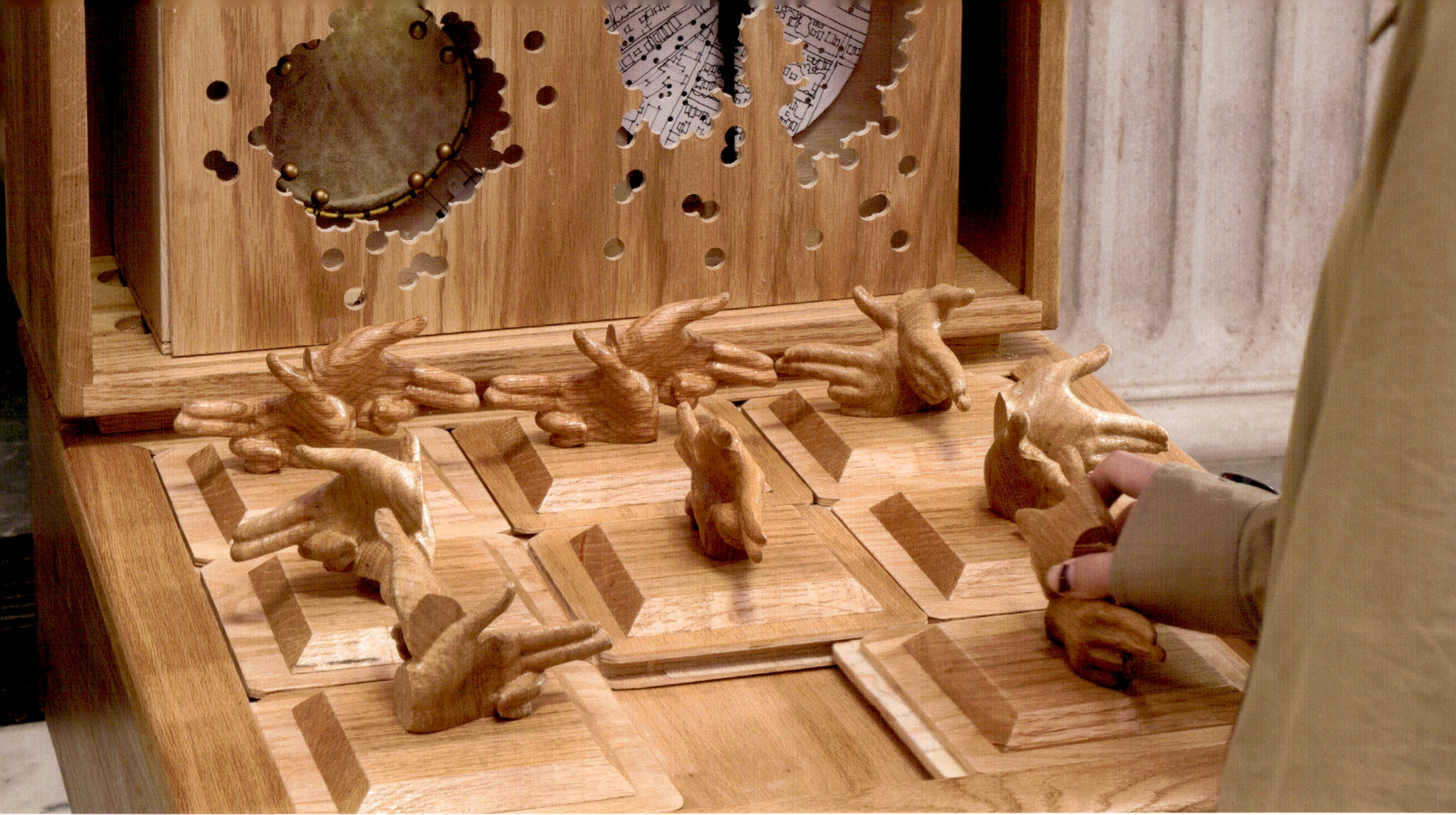

the West, local and state authorities, alongside private initiatives, organized to restrict through law and terror the Second Amendment rights of people of African descent in a Jim Crow defense of white supremacy. The wanton killing of Black and Indigenous peoples by today's police chillingly echoes this history of gun violence. While the Second Amendment may have adhered to individuals, its individual valence has long been in cahoots with the collective prerogatives of the original US citizenry—property-owning men racialized as white.

But guns also populate this history as tools of resistance. As the Jim Crow caste system took hold in the late nineteenth century, Black gun ownership appeared a practical necessity. Anti-lynching activist Ida B. Wells-Barnett noted, "A Winchester rifle should have a place of honor in every black home, and it should be used for that protection which the law refuses to give." With the Civil Rights and Black Power movements of the mid-twentieth century emerged armed groups, such as Robert Williams's Monroe, NC, chapter of the NAACP and the Louisiana-based Deacons for Defense, organized in favor of racial justice. Perhaps the most iconic embodiment of the Second Amendment's radical promise was the Black Panther Party for Self-Defense. Point seven of the party's Ten Point Program, released in 1967, reads: "We believe we can end police brutality in our Black community by organizing Black self-defense groups that are dedicated to defending our Black community from racist police oppression and brutality. The Second Amendment of the Constitution of the United States gives us the right to bear arms. We therefore believe that all Black people should arm themselves for self-defense."

The Black Panther Party's Second Amendment, rooted in defense of Black communities, was in some ways a long way from the *Heller* decision, but both sprang from a profound shift unleashed in the 1960s. Galvanized by the specter of Black Power, rising civil-rights gains, and increasing urban unrest during that decade, the "War on Crime" remade American politics and American society through no-holds-barred policies that criminalized Black boys and men and inaugurated, according to Michelle Alexander, a "New Jim Crow."[2] As legal scholar Jonathan Simon notes, the Second Amendment underwent a "constitutional moment" as it became cast as a tool, alongside the bloated prison system and the militarized police, to fight crime at all costs.[3] By the 1970s, the National Rifle Association set forth its own version of "tough-on-crime" politics, embracing a hard-line defense of the Second Amendment as Americans' ultimate safeguard against the threat of criminality—often portrayed through xenophobic and racist tropes—amid the societal and governmental failures that left Americans otherwise defenseless.

By the early 2010s, "self-defense" would surpass "hunting" as the number one reason Americans owned guns.[4] Today, roughly three-quarters of Americans oppose a handgun ban—a reversal from the 1960s, the last time most supported it.[5] Indeed, during 2020, Americans flocked to gun stores under pandemic uncertainty, police violence, economic collapse, and democratic insecurity. Data from the National Shooting Sports Foundation suggest more than 8 million people bought guns for the first time in 2020, while armed groups across the political spectrum—from antimask protesters to factions of the Black Lives Matter movement—turned to guns for political voice and personal protection.[6]

The Second Amendment's "tough-on-crime" recalibration, however, was not inevitable. After all, the threat of gun violence—everyday forms of gun violence *and* high-profile assassinations—galvanized the US Congress to pass the 1968 Gun Control Act. Since 1968, over 1.5 million people have died from gunshot wounds in the US, but with a handful of exceptions, these figures have failed to incite federal movement on gun policy. Despite aggregate declines since the 1990s, gun violence in underserved communities of color, including police killings of Black and Indigenous peoples, persists at unconscionable levels. And national gun homicide may be rising once again, with data suggesting as much as a 25 percent increase over 2020.[7] The surge of gun violence in 2020 and into 2021 threatened a "new" post-pandemic "normal."

The twenty-seven words of the Second Amendment enshrine one of the most controversial and consequential constitutional rights. Indeed, on the eve of the opening of this exhibit, the US Supreme Court handed down its ruling in *New York Rifle & Pistol Association, Inc. v. Bruen* explicitly extending the Second Amendment's purview to include gun carry outside the home. The Second Amendment appears throughout US history as an invitation and an incitement. It has served as a means of pledging allegiance to a long-standing American ideal of rugged individualism—an ideal that has justified violence, oppression, and white supremacy; provided fodder for reimagining freedom and reclaiming justice; and served as a stopgap of security when all else fails, as it so often does amid the frailty of the American social safety net. The social life of guns reminds us that the Second Amendment—an individual right to keep and bear arms by US Supreme Court ruling—is what we make of it, and that its history, for better or for worse, is still being written.

---

2. Michelle Alexander, *The New Jim Crow: Mass Incarceration in the Age of Colorblindness* (New York: The New Press, 2020).

3. Jonathan Simon, "Gun Rights and the Constitutional Significance of Violent Crime," *William & Mary Bill of Rights Journal* (2003): 12, 335.

4. "Why Own a Gun? Protection Is Now Top Reason," Pew Research Center, March 12, 2013, https://www.pewresearch.org/politics/2013/03/12/why-own-a-gun-protection-is-now-top-reason.

5. "Guns," Gallup, https://news.gallup.com/poll/1645/guns.aspx.

6. Joe Bartozzi, "Taking Stock of Record-Setting 2020 Firearm Year," January 7, 2021, https://www.nssf.org/taking-stock-of-record-setting-2020-firearm-year.

7. "2020 Was a Record-Breaking Year for Gun-Related Deaths in the U.S.," NPR, January 3, 2021, https://www.npr.org/2021/01/03/952969760/2020-was-a-record-breaking-year-for-gun-related-deaths-in-the-u-s.

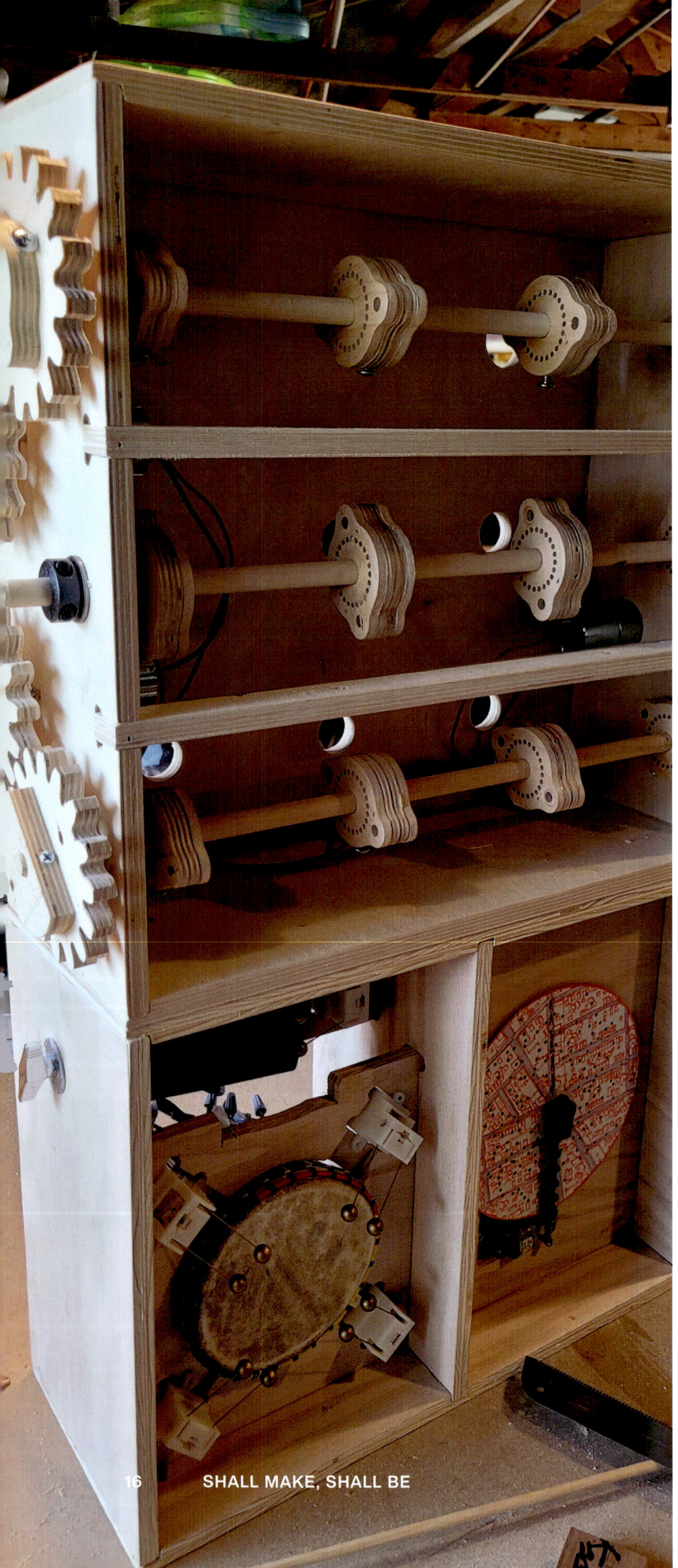

ARTIST COMMENTARY

Andy Malone
Standoff

Standoff is a physical combination puzzle that can be solved by sliding eight tiles into the correct configuration. Each tile features two carved fingers pointed in a "gun hand" pose. The player manipulates the tiles so the fingers are pointed at each other, creating a balance, or a standoff. This represents my ideal interpretation of the Second Amendment: a means to create equilibrium.

Once the puzzle is solved, buttons on the front of the table are activated and may be pressed to trigger mechanical movements in the back box. These movements serve as a commentary on American gun culture, evoking the complicated legacy of the Second Amendment. Before a player leaves the table, the puzzle should be scrambled for the next player.

I approached this project by first examining the idealistic notions behind the Second Amendment and then juxtaposing them with reflections on the impact of modern gun culture.

A standoff is a form of equilibrium.

The Second Amendment was included in the Bill of Rights to protect the right of American citizens to legally own and use firearms. The founders correlated "arms" with perseverance and independence. The Second Amendment renders any prohibitive regulations on arms unconstitutional. For early Americans, being armed was a way to maintain equilibrium between the people and entities that might do them harm, be they criminals, wildlife, an invading army, or municipal overreach. In this utopian vision, the right to bear arms maintains a level playing field.

A standoff only occurs if both sides are balanced.

In *Standoff*, the ideal interpretation of the "right to bear arms" is abstracted in a sliding puzzle. Each of the sliding tiles incorporates carved hands pointed in the "gun pose," an almost universally understood gesture. To solve the puzzle, the viewer must manipulate the tiles so that the fingers all point at each other, thus creating a counterbalance, or a standoff.

A standoff is the uneasy peace created by the threat of mutually assured destruction.

Once the puzzle is complete, motorized mechanisms can be activated by pushing buttons on the front of the cabinet, a bridge between theory and actuality. The abstracted simplicity gives way to a complicated legacy of racism, classism, and cruelty. One of the mechanisms features an accidental musical composition entitled "Aversion Therapy," which addresses my personal relationship with firearms.

A standoff is a contest in which there is no winner.

Standoff is about appreciating the spirit of the Second Amendment while despising gun violence. It is about reconciling American mythology with American brutality.

Huge thanks to Jeff Smith (SmithMade), Brian Covington (Proto Cast Inc.), Niko Solomos (Display Group), Ed O'Toole (George P. Johnson), Wendy Marvel (FlipBooKit), David Smiertka, Brad Litwin, and JP Kelly for their fabrication support and expertise. I would also like to send love to my wife, Elaine, and my children, Julia and Martin, for their patience, encouragement, and inspiration.

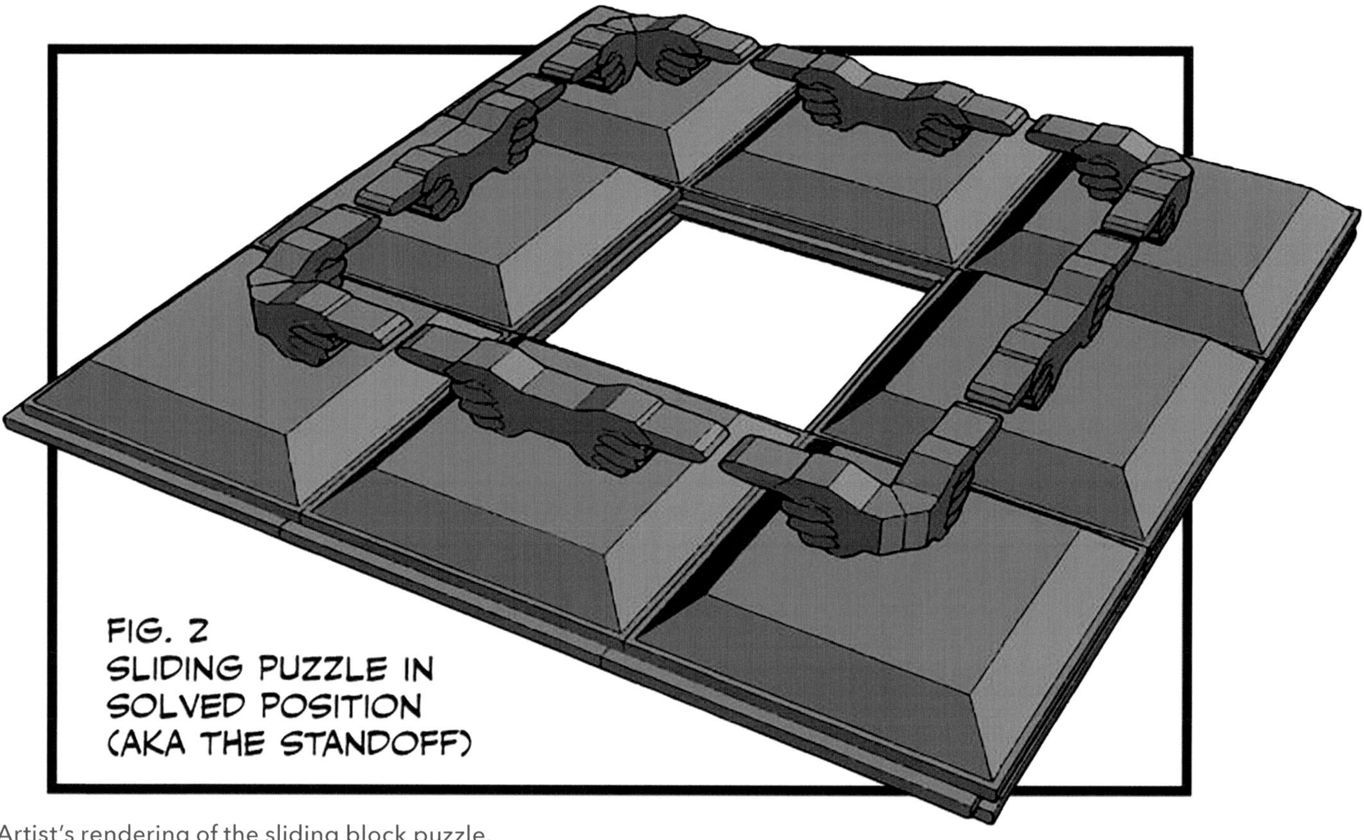

Artist's rendering of the sliding block puzzle.

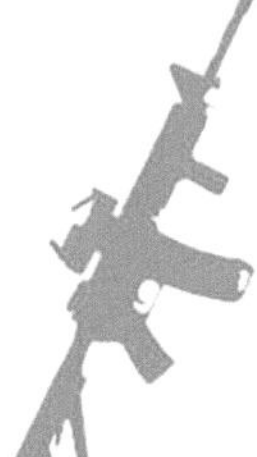

THE ACCIDENTAL MUSICAL COMPOSITION IS DERIVED FROM THE BULLET PATTERN OF AN AK-15. THE BULLET HOLE LOCATIONS TRIGGER MALLETS WHICH STRIKE AN AFRICAN TONGUE DRUM.

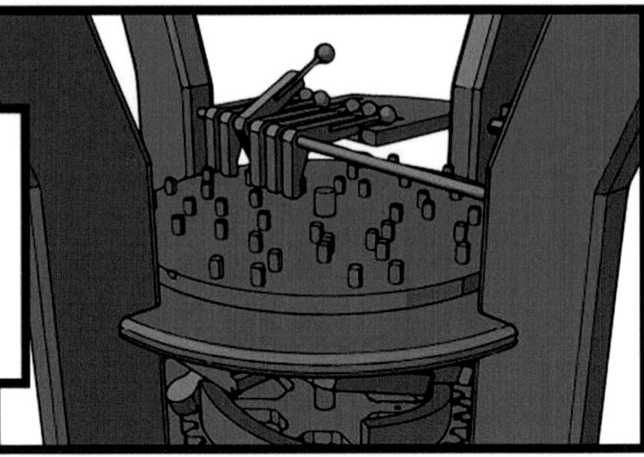

FIG. 5
STACCATO COMPOSITION

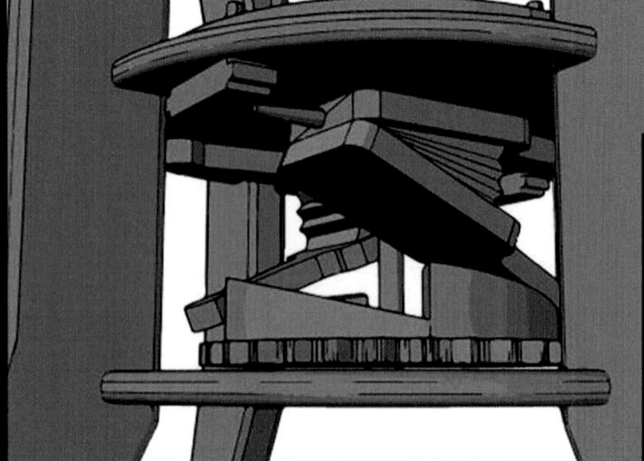

FIG. 6
LEGATO COMPOSITION

THIS STACCATO COMPOSITION IS JUXTAPOSED WITH A SECONDARY LEGATO TONE CREATED BY BELLOWS AND A HARMONICA. THIS SECONDARY TONE REPRESENTS THE FIRE RATE OF A REVOLUTIONARY ERA RIFLE COMMONLY USED IN 1791 (WHEN THE SECOND AMENDMENT WAS ADOPTED.)

THE AK-15 FIRES ROUGHLY 45 ROUNDS PER MINUTE VERSUS THE REVOLUTIONARY RIFLE WHICH ONLY FIRES 3 ROUNDS PER MINUTE.

THE COMPOSITION SERVES AS AN AURAL MEDITATION ON THE DIFFERENCES IN FIREARM TECHNOLOGY OVER THE PAST 230 YEARS.

EVERY NOTE IS A BULLET FIRED

"STANDOFF" ADDRESSES THE DICHOTOMY OF APPRECIATING THE SPIRIT OF THE SECOND AMENDMENT WHILE DESPISING GUN VIOLENCE.

"STANDOFF" IS MY ATTEMPT TO RECONCILE AMERICAN MYTHOLOGY WITH AMERICAN BRUTALITY.

"I LOVE AMERICA MORE THAN ANY OTHER COUNTRY IN THIS WORLD, AND, EXACTLY FOR THIS REASON, I INSIST ON THE RIGHT TO CRITICIZE HER PERPETUALLY"

JAMES BALDWIN, AMERICAN AUTHOR AND POET

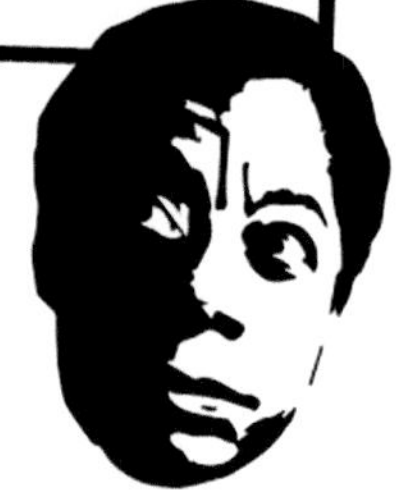

Early concept art from Andy Malone's proposal for the work. Malone originally conceived of the work as drum-shaped, emphasizing the percussive conclusion to the slide puzzle.

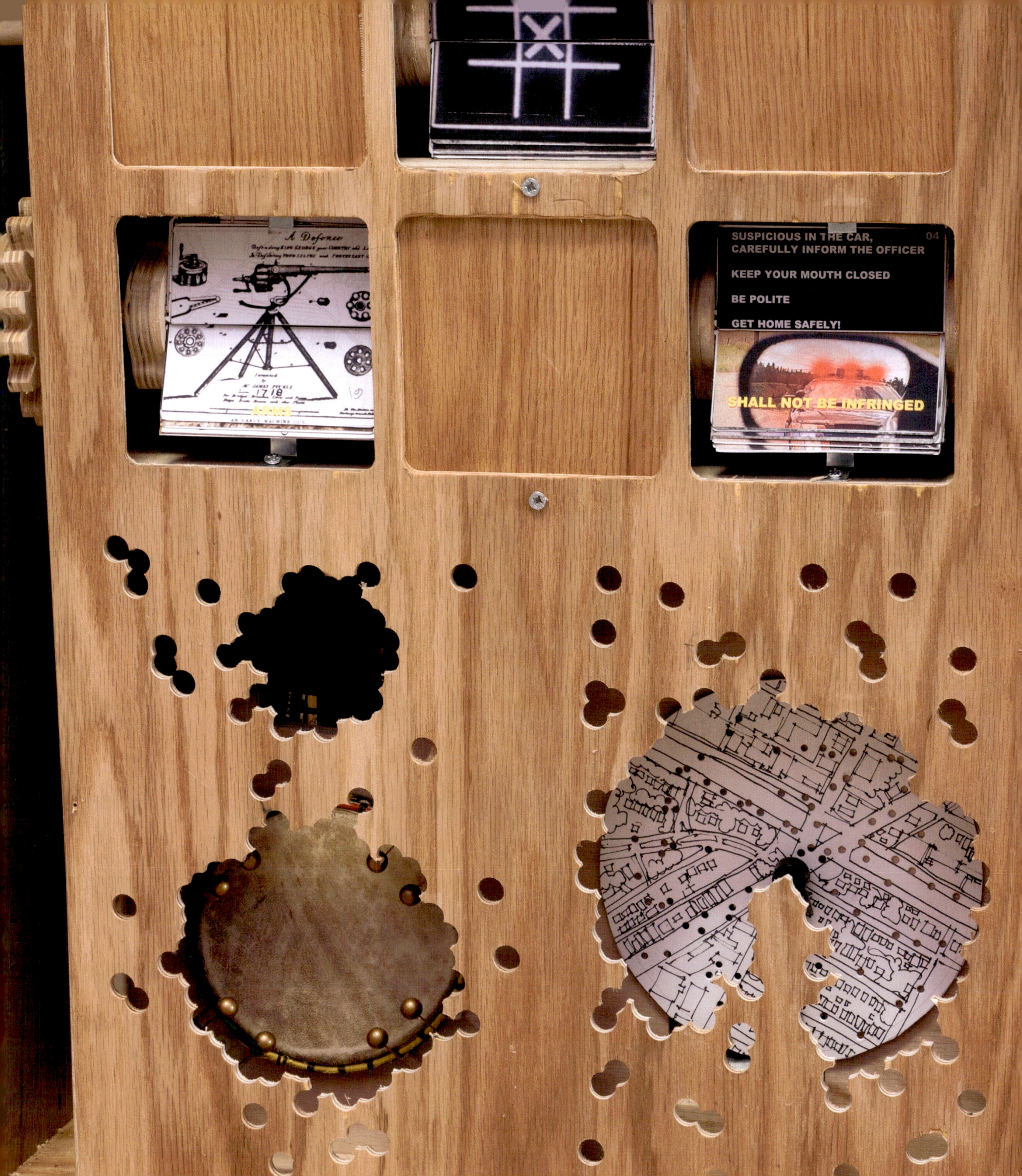
A Defence
Invented by Mr JAMES PUCKLE
1718
AN EARLY MACHINE GUN
SUSPICIOUS IN THE CAR,
CAREFULLY INFORM THE OFFICER
04
KEEP YOUR MOUTH CLOSED
BE POLITE
GET HOME SAFELY!
SHALL NOT BE INFRINGED

One working mental model of how, exactly, guns work is based on the loading of a revolver: someone loads six bullets into the cylinder, holds the gun by the handle, gives it a flick to spin the cylinder, then a flick in the other direction to reseat the cylinder in the frame, points the barrel toward the target, and pulls the trigger, which releases the hammer, which in turn fires a bullet out of the cylinder, through the barrel, and toward the target. Or maybe your understanding comes from a more contemporary gun with a magazine: bullets are one by one fed into a clip, which is in turn seated in the handle, enabling each bullet to be propelled into the chamber for firing.

The simplicity of these mechanical devices frames how we think all guns work, more or less. Guns, in other words, are yet another deadly "black box" in our lives, the complexity of which is masked by the simplistic model we use to understand them. This is a predicament of our post-mechanical, post-information world: we have made machines to augment us, to make us faster, smarter, more powerful. But do these machines pull this off? Do they pull this off in ways that better our lives and that don't make them worse? Do these black boxes enhance both the good and the bad in the human condition?

Andy Malone's *Standoff* presents a literal and figurative Rube Goldberg-meets-slide-puzzle conception of the goings-on inside a gun and within the consequences of eight gun-wielding people. Players slide the puzzle pieces seeking the correct configuration of pointing fingers. The pointing-finger-mounted puzzle squares in turn trigger gears, levers, and pistons in order to enact mechanical and social tensions that lead to the brandishing of these violent black boxes. The mechanical complexity of the work nods to both the absurdity of machines holding such sway over us and the inevitability that black boxes, once in existence, seem unstoppable.

When certain conditions are met, and the puzzle pieces are in the right order, the work strikes a chord—once more, literally and figuratively. The sharp strike of a fired gun makes real the power of the black box, unmasking its violent purpose. Even for those keen on guns, this sound is too much. Protective devices shield the shooter from this striking reality. This sound is the most literal aspect of *Standoff*, bringing us back from the mechanical wonder of Malone's craft skills to the jarring reality of these black boxes that augment humanity's violent instincts.

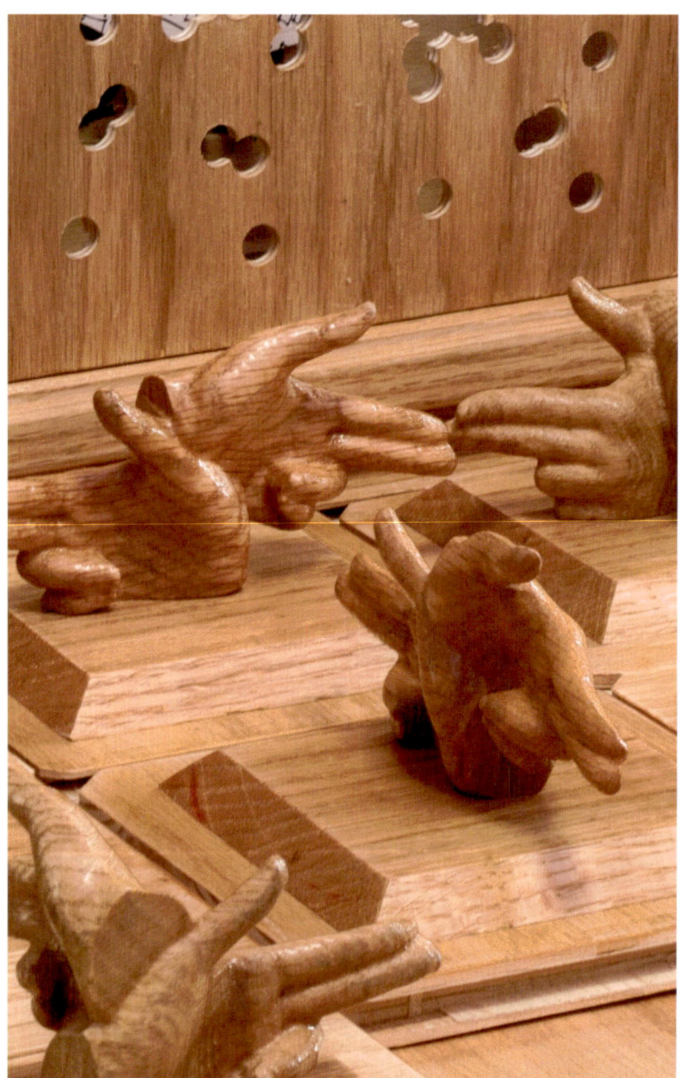

THE THIRD AMENDMENT

No Soldier shall, in time of peace be quartered in any house, without the consent of the Owner, nor in time of war, but in a manner to be prescribed by law.

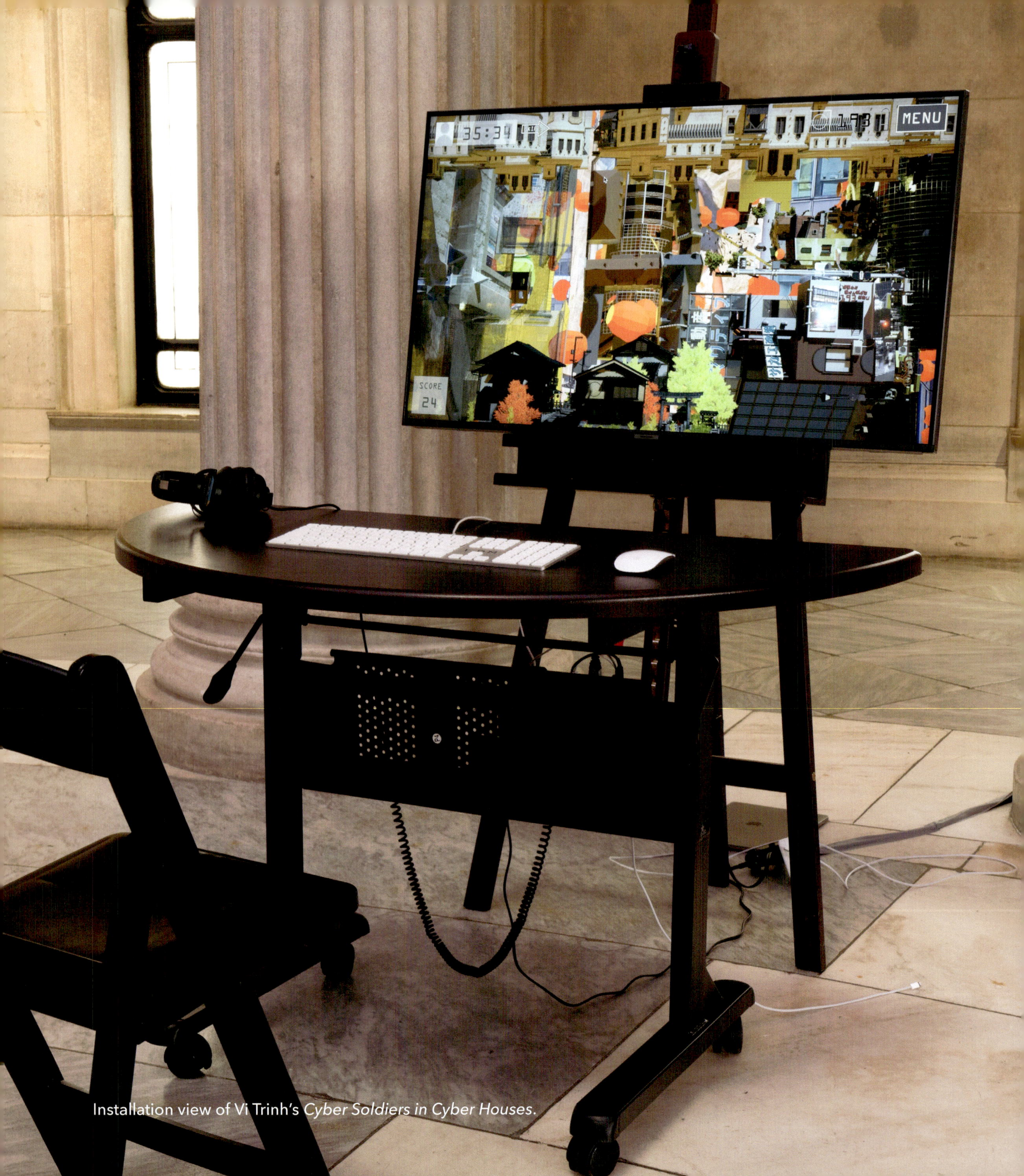

Installation view of Vi Trinh's *Cyber Soldiers in Cyber Houses*.

Vi Trinh
Cyber Soldiers in Cyber Houses, 2022
Computer software with video, sound
Dimensions variable

INTERROGATING THE THIRD AMENDMENT

ALEXANDER ZHANG

JD-PhD student, Yale University

> Whether as a rhetorical device, thought experiment, or legal protection, the Third Amendment may not see much time in court, but it has hardly drawn its last breath.

Death inspires dreams of rebirth. As a matter of law, the Third Amendment of the US Constitution mostly died as soon as it was born, and ever since, it has been forgotten and dismissed but sometimes, surprisingly, rehabilitated.

Although courts today are unlikely to revive the Third Amendment, it nevertheless raises important contemporary questions about the role of government, the nature of privacy, and the consequences of militarization. Its text is narrow, limiting its application to specific scenarios and types of people. But the reasons people once opposed quartering were many.

Angst about the quartering of troops had already been present by the time the American Revolution began. In England, for instance, criticisms against standing armies had led Parliament to enact the Anti-Quartering Act in 1679. These negative sentiments continued in the British North American colonies, where local officials tried to reject requests to quarter British soldiers. As historian John McCurdy has written, a growing sense that the home was a private space led people to particularly dislike the idea of having soldiers in their houses. Soldiers brought dangers to the home. They broke things. They sexually assaulted women. As smallpox epidemics raged on, they could also spread disease. The eventual ratification of the Third Amendment in 1791 could help protect against these ills, but by then, the American Revolution was over.[8]

In the following two centuries, the Third Amendment rarely saw glory. The Third Amendment allowed for quartering in "time of war" as long as it was "prescribed by law," and during both the War of 1812 and the Civil War, American soldiers occupied private

---

8. William S. Fields and David T. Hardy, "The Third Amendment and the Issue of the Maintenance of Standing Armies: A Legal History," *American Journal of Legal History* 35, no. 4 (Oct. 1991): 393–431; John Gilbert McCurdy, *Quarters: The Accommodation of the British Army and the Coming of the American Revolution* (Ithaca, NY: Cornell University Press, 2019), esp. 10–49, 236–37.

homes. As the twentieth century arrived, the Third Amendment was clearly becoming something of a museum artifact. US Representative Sol Bloom asserted in 1926, "It is hard for a modern youth to realize the importance and even the meaning of the Third Amendment," since "he has seldom heard of [quartering]; and, if he has, he sees nothing wrong in allowing it." By 1930, one writer was claiming that the Third Amendment "is obsolete now."[9]

But when people did remember and invoke the Third Amendment, rare as this was, the amendment became an ideological weapon rather than a legal tool to stop quartering itself. After Lindley Miller Garrison, a secretary of war under President Woodrow Wilson, proposed to expand the United States' standing army in the mid-1910s, one writer objected because the Third Amendment showed that "our forefathers were so strongly moved by the evils of a standing army as to enter these protests so formally." Some invoked the Third Amendment as a symbol of Americanism, others as a check on American exceptionalism. In 1936, one writer explained that whereas the United States had been protected by the Third Amendment, "Hitler brownshirts conduct modern dragonnades in Germany." Four years later, amid reports of Nazis meeting in New Jersey, one person claimed that even though "bundites, communists, camorrasites, and other parasites who crowd patriotic citizens back from the table of opportunity . . . are protected by the bill of rights," the Third Amendment might somehow bar them from staying in the United States. After World War II ended, one writer invoked the Third Amendment not to praise the United States but to criticize how American soldiers abroad had been "throwing German civilians out of their homes and setting up luxurious living quarters for themselves and their wives."[10]

Courts have similarly invoked the Third Amendment for broader purposes. In a famous 1965 case called *Griswold v. Connecticut*, the US Supreme Court used it to help show that the Constitution included protections of people's privacy. Other courts, as legal scholar Tom Bell has written, have referenced the amendment to comment on the uses of subpoenas, the relationship between militaries and civilians, the nature of constitutional interpretation, and more.[11]

That doesn't mean that courts haven't specifically looked at potential violations of the Third Amendment too. Most notably, in a 1982 case called *Engblom v. Carey*, after the state of New York housed National Guard troops in the residences of correctional officers, the Second Circuit Court of Appeals found that the correctional officers had a "legitimate expectation of privacy protected by the Third Amendment." The court explained that National Guard troops counted as "soldiers," that the correctional officers counted as "owners," and that the Third Amendment applied at the state and not just the federal level. More recently, a federal court in 2015 rejected a Third Amendment claim involving Nevada police officers' occupation of a private home, holding that municipal police officers were not "soldiers."

The scope of the Third Amendment and whether it can and should be used in litigation for purposes other than the unconsented residence of military troops in private homes is ultimately a question of which methods one should use to interpret the Constitution. The modern applications of a narrow reading are few, and the desirability of broad interpretations is debatable.

---

9. Tom W. Bell, "The Third Amendment: Forgotten but Not Gone," *William & Mary Bill of Rights Journal* 2, no. 1 (1993): 136–40; "President's Help Sought for Film of Constitution," *New York Times*, November 21, 1926, 14; "Voice of the People," *Indianapolis News*, May 28, 1930, 6.

10. "The Standing Army," *Des Moines Register*, October 27, 1915, 6; Liberties of an American, *Chicago Daily Tribune*, June 7, 1936, 14; "Plotting and Publishing by Alien Agents and Agitators," *Salt Lake Tribune*, September 3, 1940, 8; Julian W. Hughes, "Open Forum . . . : Our Bill of Rights: Quartering of Soldiers," *Daily Times-News*, March 29, 1949, 12.

11. Bell, "The Third Amendment," 141.

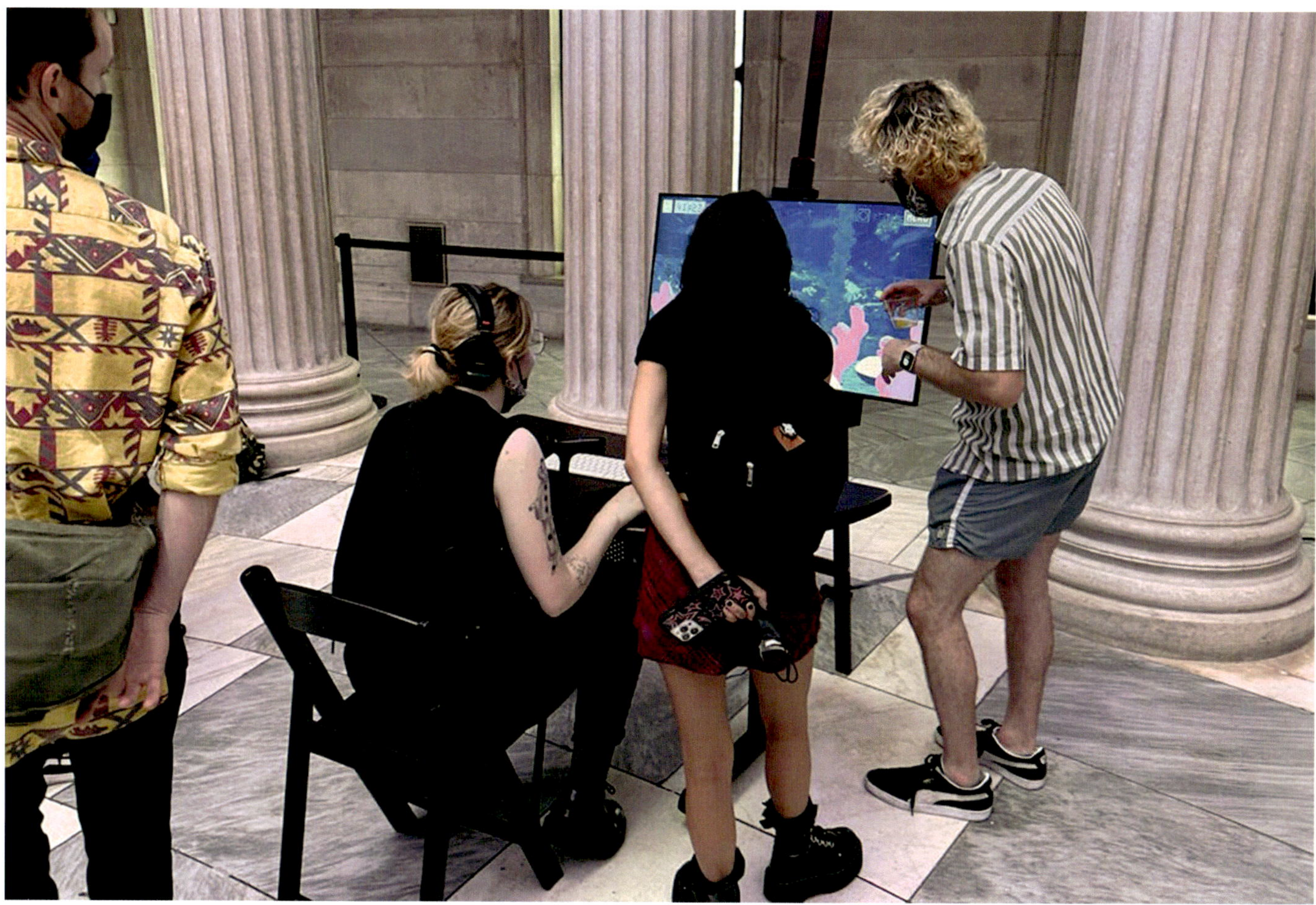

But the amendment's legacy endures; one only needs to recall the spectacular image of National Guard troops living in the halls of the US Capitol—and not in private homes—after rioters stormed the Capitol in January 2021.

Regardless of its usefulness in litigation, the Third Amendment lives on, just as it did in the twentieth century, as a thought-provoking tool and orthogonal intellectual entryway into important contemporary questions. Commentators have drawn on it to examine the militarization of police, legality of wiretapping, compensation for government takings of private property, and much more. In an age in which American warfare persists without formal declarations of war, the Third Amendment invites us to ask what it means for a country to be "in time of peace" rather than "in time of war."[12] Whether as a rhetorical device, thought experiment, or legal protection, the Third Amendment may not see much time in court, but it has hardly drawn its last breath.

---

12. See, for example, Samantha A. Lovin, "Everyone Forgets About the Third Amendment: Exploring the Implications on Third Amendment Case Law of Extending Its Prohibitions to Include Actions by State Police Officers," *William & Mary Bill of Rights Journal* 23, no. 2 (2014): 529–57; Tom W. Bell, "'Property' in the Constitution: The View from the Third Amendment," *William & Mary Bill of Rights Journal* 20, no. 4 (2012): 1243–76; Josh Dugan, "When Is a Search Not a Search? When It's a Quarter: The Third Amendment, Originalism, and NSA Wiretapping," *Georgetown Law Journal* 97, no. 2 (2009): 555–58.

ARTIST COMMENTARY

Vi Trinh

Cyber Soldiers in Cyber Houses

Cyber Soldiers in Cyber Houses is a digital multimedia eye-spy game spanning over thirty rooms with narration by two AI home assistants. After a future cyber 9/11-esque attack, the US government has increased cyber surveillance on all citizens. In this AI-assisted home, the player races against time to debug their house, finding the hidden items or bugs in each room before the game ends. Each room is attached to a Person of Interest who will be compromised if the player does not find the bugs. There is an option for the player to skip the room and move on to the next one. However, skipping a room comes at a risk. If the player has not found enough bugs to clear the room, the Person of Interest may be compromised and points will be added to the player's score. When the

timer runs out, the game automatically ends and the remaining points are tallied and added to the player's score. The scores for all the players are displayed on an adjacent screen. The player should aim for a low score and must balance time management and risk to get the best possible outcome.

Cyber Soldiers in Cyber Houses explores the implications of the Third Amendment on digital privacy. Through AI dialogue, the game examines the application of our current laws and values on emerging technology as well as the problems inherent in technology, metadata, and mass surveillance that amplify current socioeconomic inequalities. Today, rather than soldiers, we have drones; instead of spies, we have malware. *Cyber Soldiers in Cyber Houses* examines the

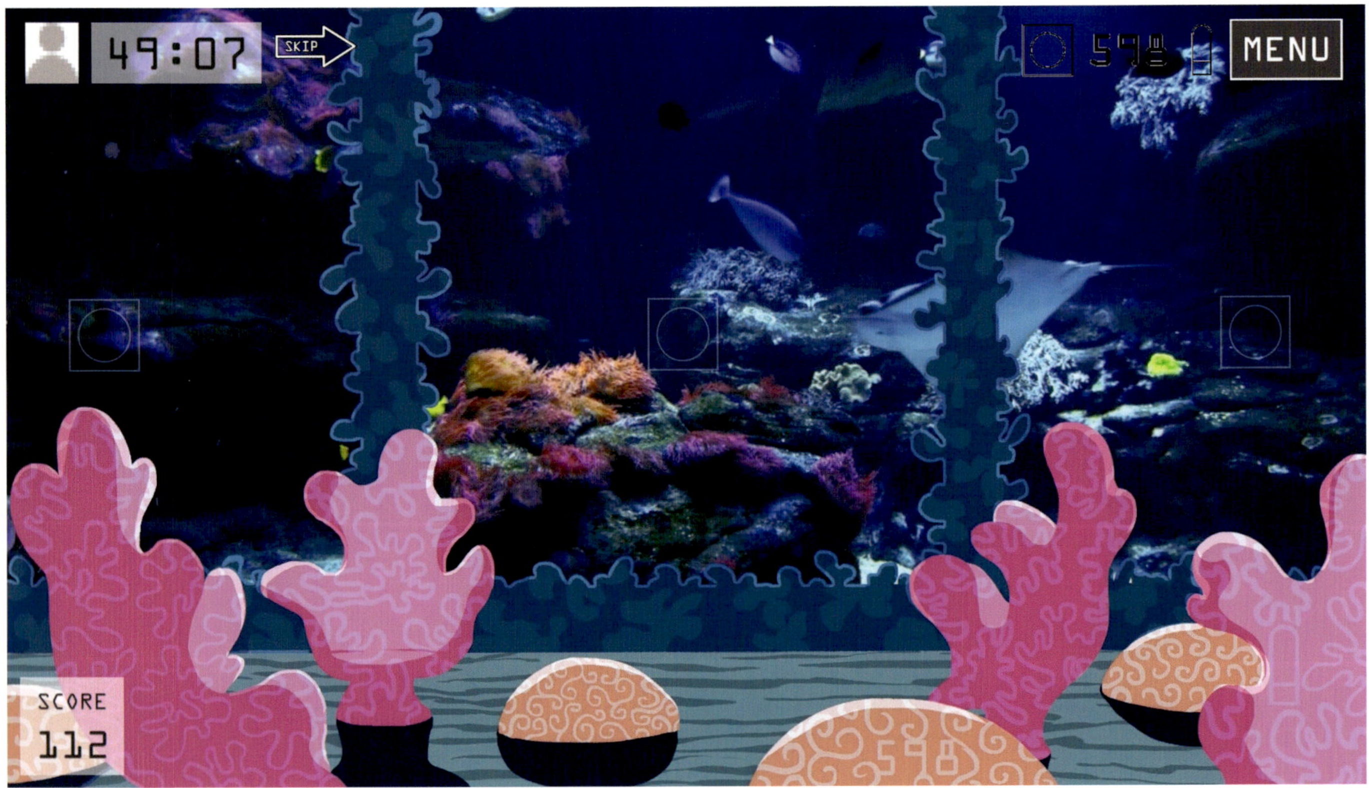

future relationship between the government and its people in the advent of stronger technology and our increased reliance on it.

The Third Amendment is the entryway to larger and more fundamental questions about privacy, the connection between the military and private companies, and the unprecedented power new technology gives the government and the hidden nature of that power. The game aims to arm the viewer with information in order to allow them to form their own conclusions about what they want policy to be. The mechanics of the game promote empathy toward others who might not have the time or resources to devote to their own privacy, even if the protection of others is inconvenient to the player. The game hopes to fight against technology designed for convenience that bypasses critical thinking. Technology in and of itself is an amoral tool, but sunk into a system of immorality it becomes an exponential factor in discrimination. It can, however, be reclaimed and repurposed for good.

How do we apply former structures, laws, and values to a rapidly expanding frontier of powerful technology? Data analysis on a grand scale has widened the scope of possible good and harm that large institutions can do. Big data and cyber surveillance are a constantly expanding frontier. There are still very few rules and restrictions to abide by, no one to answer to, and no checks on abuses of power. Currently we are expecting corporations and government institutions to hold their own leash. *Cyber Soldiers in Cyber Houses* shows how data and surveillance technology affected us in the past and affects us now, and asks what we are willing to allow in the future.

Special thanks to Athena Hosek for programming contributions that made the completion of this project possible.

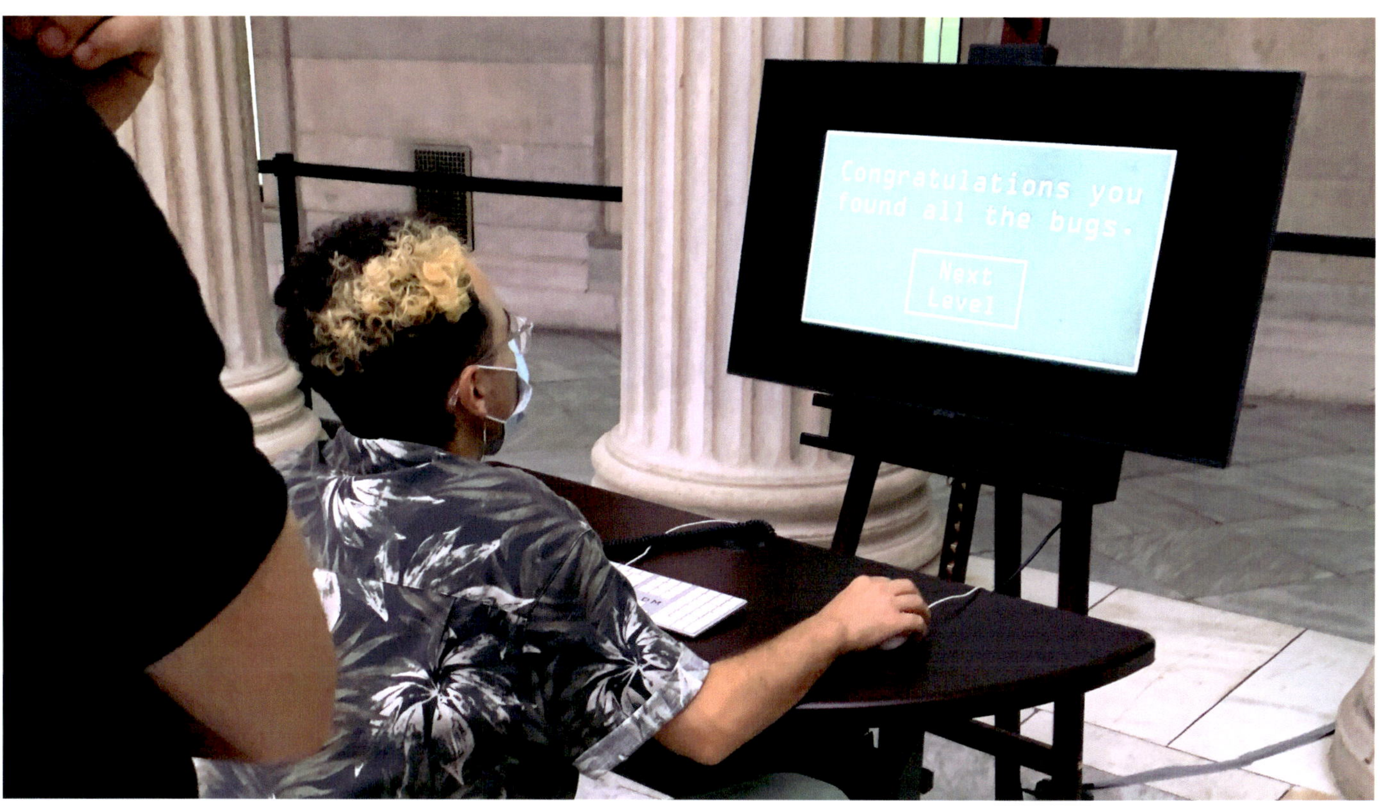

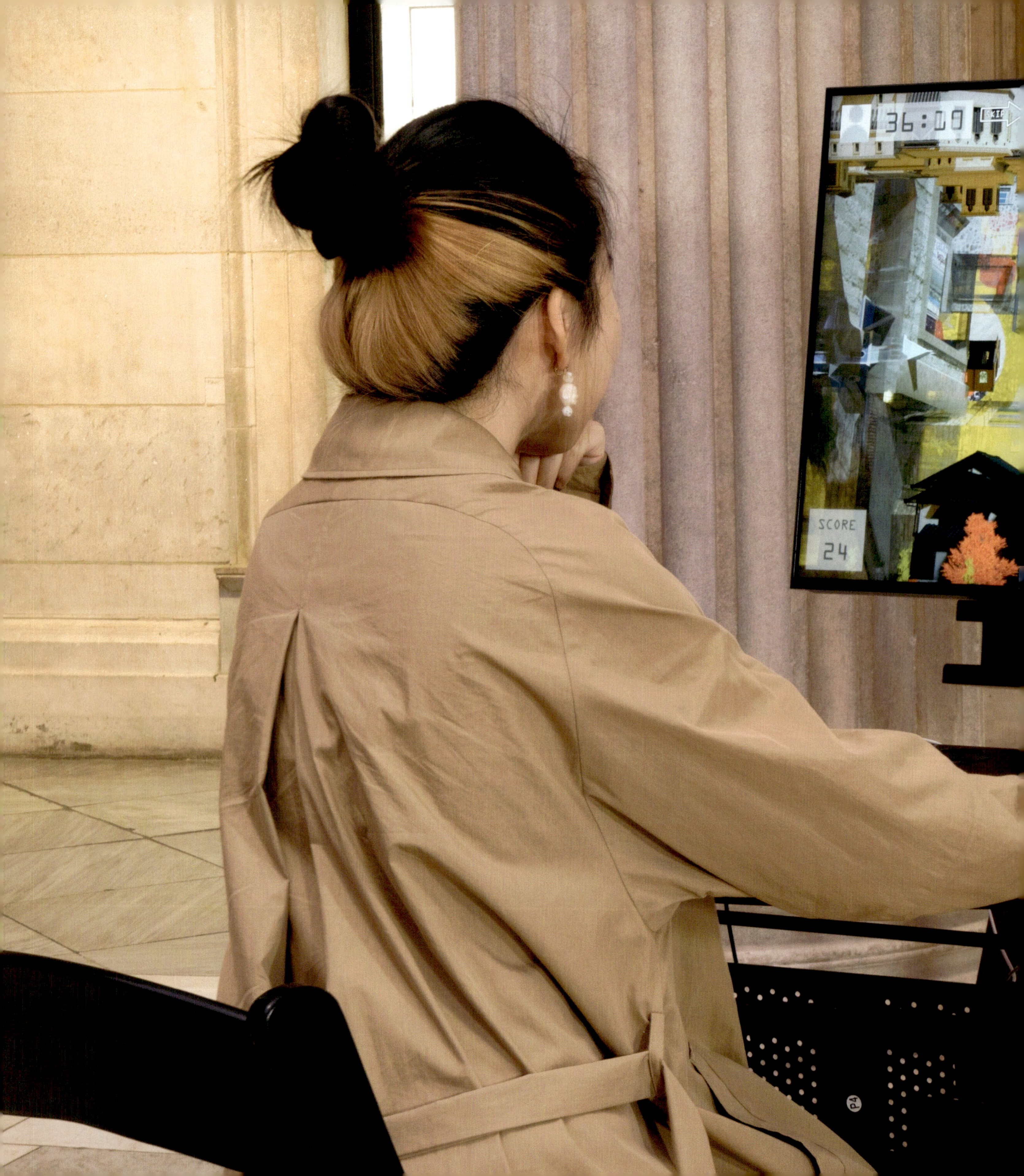

36:09
EXIT
SCORE
24

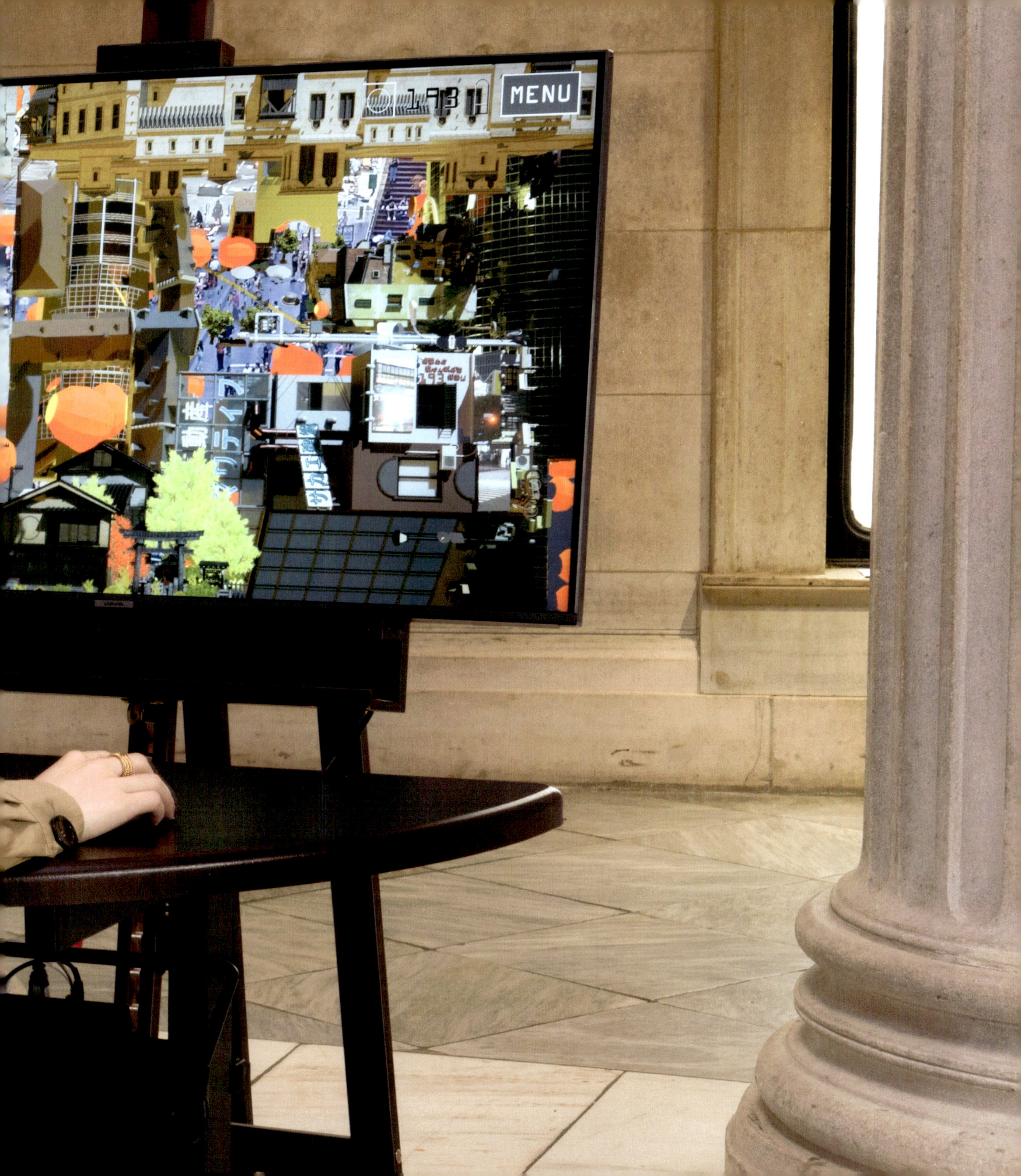
MENU

In our call for submissions for this exhibition, we anticipated a lot of interest in the First and Second Amendments, and maybe some in the Fifth, possibly the Fourth. To our surprise, the Third Amendment proved to be among the most popular, with double the number received for the Second Amendment. The underlying right described in the Third Amendment—protection from soldiers taking residence in a private home—feels distant, even quaint. Even if seldom referenced in court proceedings, the Third Amendment remains present in more colloquial contexts. While we have not had reason to literally house military representatives of the federal government in our homes, the broader implications of privacy from the federal government falls within popular understandings of the Third Amendment. More specifically, popular interpretations assume the Third Amendment affords privacy from government in domestic spaces. Inherent in this is the presumption that the federal government cannot trump local and state jurisdictions in a broad array of situations.

It is from this vantage that Vi Trinh speculates on the internet as a site for privacy from government intrusion. This is not a big leap. Indeed, much of what we recognize as the internet originated with ARPANET (US Advanced Research Projects Agency Network), a project launched in 1969 with funding by the US military. It was not until 1983 that the domain name system opened the ARPANET for applications beyond the military. A year later, the science fiction author William Gibson introduced the term *cyberspace*, creating a spatial understanding of the internet and establishing a model for comprehending the otherwise shapeless network.

In *Cyber Soldiers in Cyber Houses*, players solve hidden-object puzzles in which the player locates household infringements on cyber privacy contained within the images. True to the genre, each puzzle presents the player with a space—typically a room, filled with thematic furnishings, objects, and inhabitants. The player's goal is to find all instances of a number, a microphone, and a camera in the space. Some instances of these objects are easily identified, others more obscured. Later in the game, the spaces shift to amorphous representations of cyberspace. Mechanically, the genre emphasizes pattern identification and visual acuity. Within Trinh's work, the genre operates metaphorically: Can we see the potential for intrusion via the increasingly present "smart" appliances, alarm systems, digital personal assistants, and all manner of internet-enabled devices we bring into our homes?

As the player moves through Trinh's puzzles, the traditional physicality of objects in the hidden-object puzzle become increasingly abstract within speculative imaginings of cyberspace. When the quartered soldiers are no longer physically present, how are our rights to domestic privacy preserved?

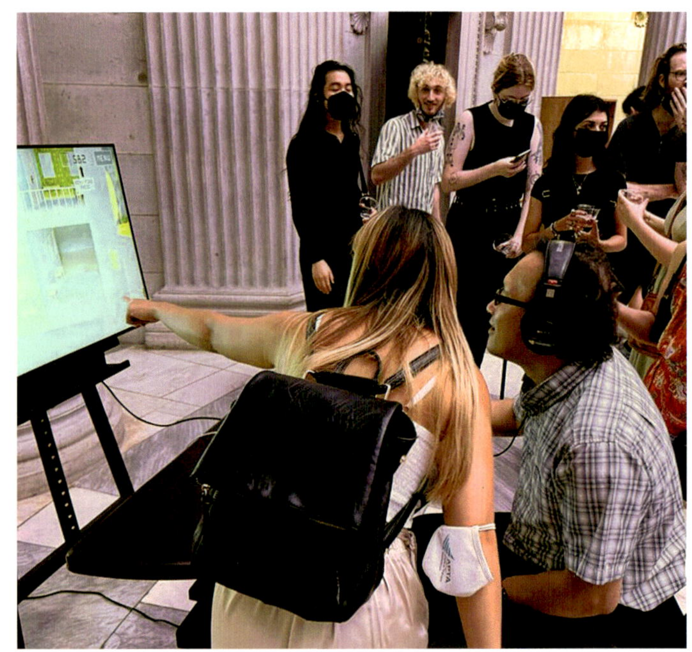

THE FOURTH AMENDMENT

The right of the people to be secure in their persons, houses, papers, and effects, against unreasonable searches and seizures, shall not be violated, and no Warrants shall issue, but upon probable cause, supported by Oath or affirmation, and particularly describing the place to be searched, and the persons or things to be seized.

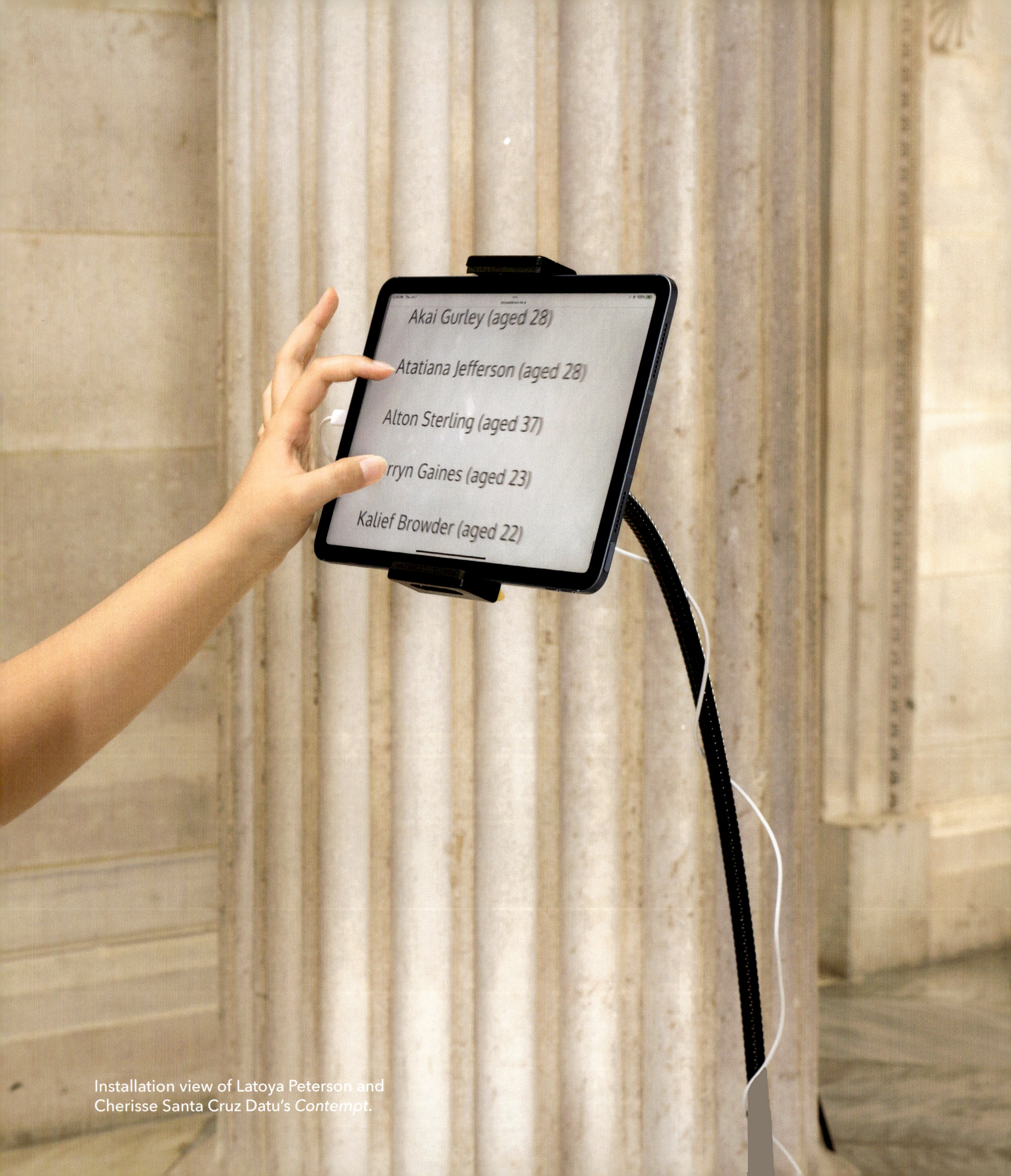

Installation view of Latoya Peterson and Cherisse Santa Cruz Datu's *Contempt*.

**Latoya Peterson and
Cherisse Santa Cruz Datu**
Contempt, 2022
Computer software with interactive play,
    self-contained on tablets, TV display
Dimensions variable

Both reasonable suspicion and probable cause are easy to produce in the age of mass criminalization.

INTERROGATING THE FOURTH AMENDMENT

JESSICA M. EAGLIN
Professor of Law, Indiana University, Bloomington

The Fourth Amendment is often considered the primary legal vehicle for protection against unwarranted surveillance. Yet its guarantee in the "right of the people to be secure . . . against unreasonable searches and seizures" has proved mostly illusory and imagined, especially for the most marginalized among us. Similarly, the guarantee that "no Warrants shall issue, but upon probable cause" has emerged as a mechanism to legitimate government intrusion into the everyday lives of everyday people.

Consider the prominence of proactive policing strategies like "stop and frisk" and racial profiling. In New York City alone, police have proactively engaged in stops and street interrogations more than 5 million times since 2002, disproportionately targeting Black and Latinx communities. Even as the evils of "stop and frisk" have gradually reached the forefront of the public

consciousness through high-impact litigation, alarming statistics on the enduring practice of proactive policing continue to be reported. For example, in 2019 alone, the NYPD reported 13,459 stops, with 59 percent of such stops being conducted on Black individuals, 29 percent on Latinx individuals, and 9 percent on white individuals. In 2020, the NYPD recorded 9,544 stops, even as a global pandemic kept New York City locked down for the greater part of the year.

The US Supreme Court paved the way for such practices through its interpretation of the Fourth Amendment. First, it set a high bar for what constitutes a search or seizure. If a police officer approaches a person, questions that person about their whereabouts, and even follows that person, it does not rise to the level of a search or seizure, thus precluding Fourth Amendment protection.

Even if interaction with police rises to the level of a

search or seizure, the courts typically determine what is "unreasonable" by balancing law enforcement's interest and society's interest in individual freedom. So, where the intrusion is minimal—such as the court's characterization of being stopped by the police as a "minor" "seizure" and being patted down by the police as a "minor" "search"—the people's interest is frequently outweighed by the interest of law enforcement so long as reasonable suspicion exists. To effectuate an arrest, the slightly higher standard of probable cause is required.

Both reasonable suspicion and probable cause are easy to produce in the age of mass criminalization. In recent decades, states and local jurisdictions have taken to criminalizing numerous kinds of nonserious behaviors and activities, from loitering to public intoxication to jaywalking and more. These behaviors are vague and ubiquitous, equipping police with broad discretion to enforce such laws selectively and disproportionately in and on poor and marginalized communities. Consequently, the legal minimums derived from the Fourth Amendment remain inadequate to stifle expanding surveillance practices.

The guarantee that home searches require a warrant fares no better. Consider the experience of Breonna Taylor. Plainclothes police entered Taylor's apartment in March 2020, at night, to serve a warrant for the arrest of her boyfriend, who did not live at the residence. Gunshots were exchanged between the police and Taylor's boyfriend. Taylor was struck by eight bullets and killed, but the police were vindicated for their entry to her home because they obtained a warrant in advance. The Fourth Amendment guaranteed procedural protection, but substantively it had nothing to say about the quality of the search of her home or the methods by which the police conducted it.

These challenges are only exacerbated as surveillance technologies expand throughout the criminal apparatus. For example, police increasingly have access to genetic DNA databases, criminal-record repositories, expansive gang databases, and predictive technologies to facilitate their surveillance practices. In the face of these developments, the very idea of what constitutes a search—does it include computer databases, access to a cloud, access to a cell phone?—remain open to debate.

To be sure, the Fourth Amendment offers some protection. As an example, consider *Carpenter v. United States* (2018). There, the US Supreme Court held that a search warrant is necessary when law enforcement seeks location data from cell-tower providers. But these protections are minimal, particularly given that the Fourth Amendment only extends to government actions or tightly correlated private actions conducted on behalf of the government. As the distinction between public and private action continues to erode with the advance of commercially developed technologies used by public actors, these limitations carry less heft.

What is more, the courts turn to the "exclusionary rule" as the primary means to enforce this right. When the government violates the Fourth Amendment, courts seek to deter police or other government actors going forward by suppressing evidence obtained in violation of the Fourth Amendment in a particular criminal case. But even then, numerous carve-outs exist whereby the evidence may still be used. Thus, if the Fourth Amendment deters at all, this right has emerged as a weak means to vindicate the people's right not to be surveilled and engaged by the police on a daily basis.

In summary, the Fourth Amendment provides illusory protections from the threat of unwarranted surveillance. If we are to begin to imagine a world where surveillance of the most marginalized is not pro forma, we will need to begin to imagine the Fourth Amendment and the broader legal landscape around policing anew in light of realities about structural marginalization and the expanding carceral state.

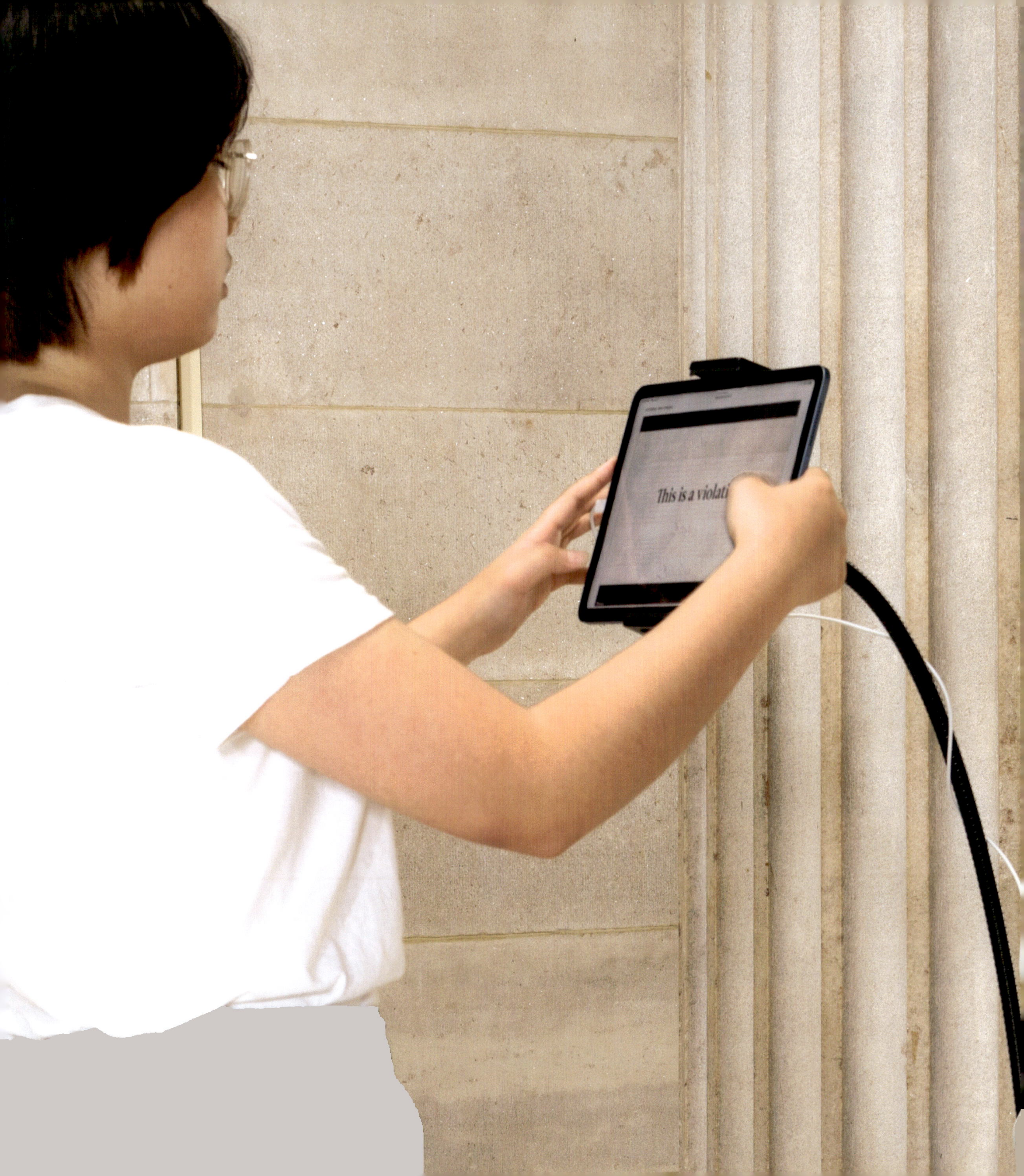
This is a violati

Contempt is a single-player interactive experience, opening with a playable reflection on the Fourth Amendment. What do these words mean? What is the emphasis? Players arrange words from the Bill of Rights on-screen. Once the amendment is complete, the screen fades to black. The player is then roused from sleep in a pitch-black room. Given a matter of seconds to understand what is happening, the player must make decisions literally in the dark, reminiscent of the experience of an unlawful search and seizure. The piece opens again on a black screen with more detail: this time the player has less than two minutes to make a life-altering decision—should they look for a flashlight? A gun? What can they do in this scenario?

The name *Contempt* holds multiple meanings in this work. Referencing both the idea of willful disobedience under the law and the contempt that Black Americans face from racially biased police, this piece hopes to have players understand the current interpretation of the Fourth Amendment, its historical significance, and its future.

Contempt is a response to the injustice of current events. On March 13, 2020, twenty-six-year-old Breonna Taylor was killed in her home. Peacefully sleeping, the Louisville-based emergency room technician had no idea police were approaching her apartment to execute a "no-knock" warrant, searching for contraband and a different suspect. The officers fired thirty-two rounds, fatally wounding Taylor and sparking an international conversation on policing and reform.

Black Lives Matter had become a rallying cry for justice years before that fateful day in Louisville, demanding equal treatment under the law for Black citizens. As an ever-growing list of names detailed a litany of injustices, the role of police practices in Taylor's death fell under a microscope. But as her death became a part of the nightly news cycle, it grew obvious that many in the United States did not see Black

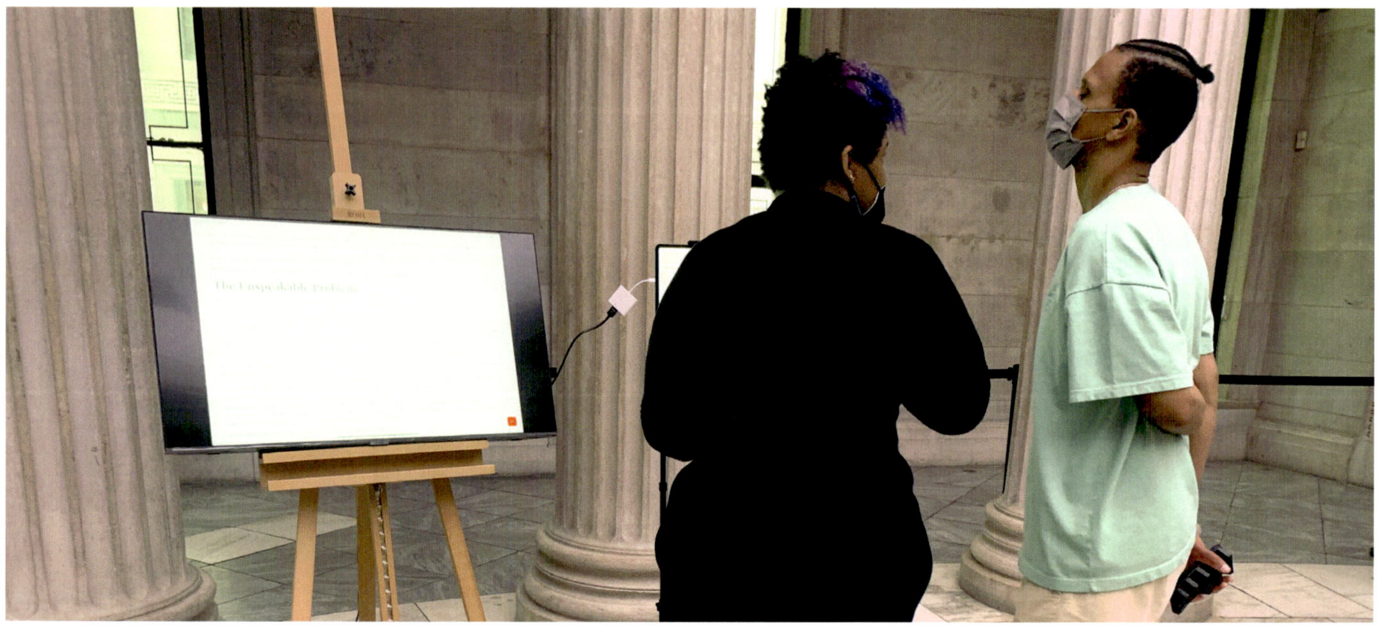

Americans as citizens with the right to equal protections under the law. Other high-profile cases, like that of thirty-two-year-old Philando Castile, who was killed by law enforcement during a traffic stop in 2016, and the chain of events that began with a 2015 traffic stop for twenty-eight-year-old Sandra Bland and ended in her death, illustrate that flagrant violations of foundational civil liberties are frequently excused depending on the race of the victim. It is clear that Black Americans are not truly protected by the explicit safeguards the Bill of Rights should afford to all citizens.

The Fourth Amendment, which provides protection against unlawful search and seizure, should receive the same full-throated defense as we see of the First and Second Amendments. But why are Black bodies seen as undeserving of the same laws and protections as other citizens? *Contempt* is designed to explore the Fourth Amendment and its protections through prose and playable experiences, examining how race and American history have influenced the interpretation and popular understanding of this amendment.

Early concept art from Latoya Peterson and Cherisse Santa Cruz Datu's proposal for the work. Peterson and Datu originally conceived of the work as projecting on a large screen but ultimately opted for a more intimate play experience.

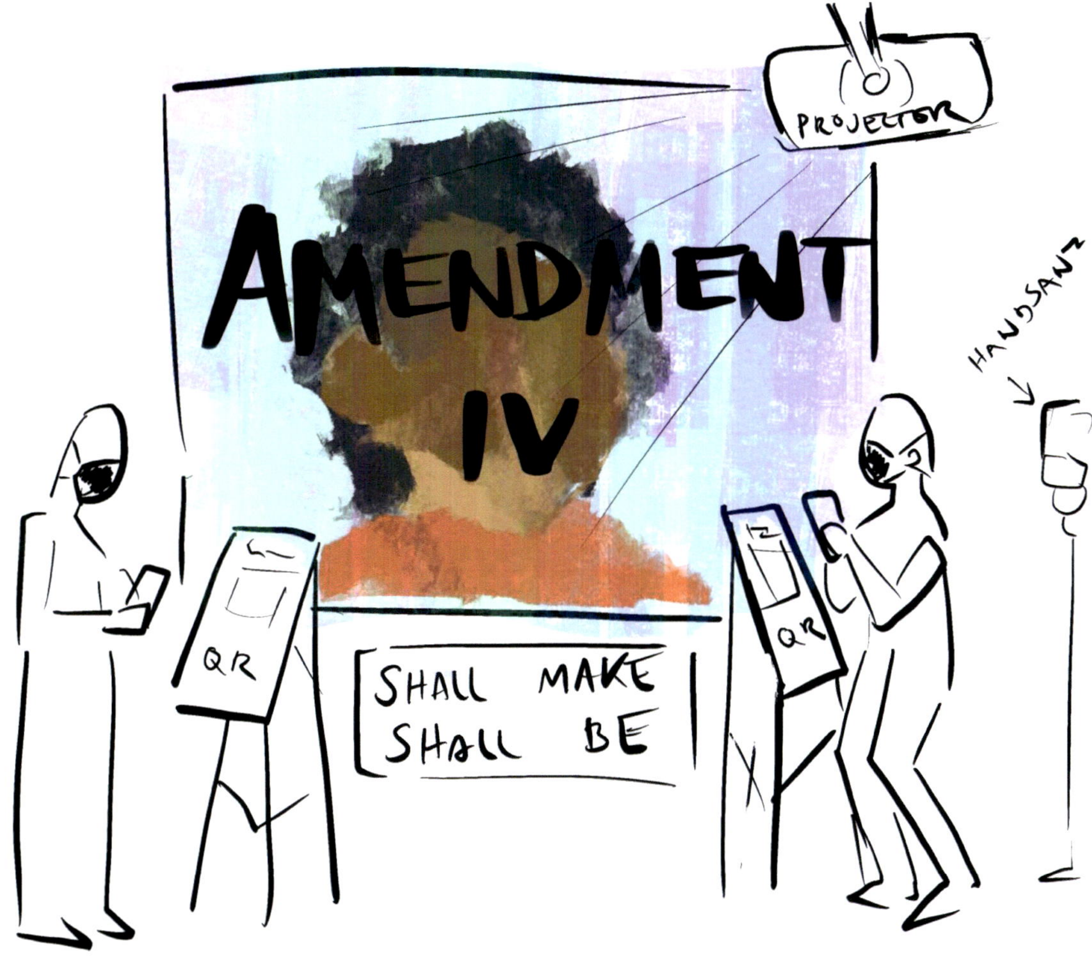

When a game's rules feel both fair and evenly applied, players develop trust—in the game and in one another. Games thrive on trust, allowing the necessary vulnerability and commitment to play. Conversely, if players don't believe everyone is playing fairly and/or upholding the agreed-upon rules, the game will break due to a lack of trust. Sometimes players think they are above the rules; sometimes players think no one will notice or care if they break the rules. Sometimes players think no one can do anything about them breaking the rules. All three of these will eventually break trust in the game.

Like games, laws are fragile ecosystems that require attention to maintain their fairness. Just because a law is written doesn't mean it will be faithfully followed any more than a game's rules will be followed by all players. The idea of "house rules" helps us think about the interpretation and upholding of laws like the Fourth Amendment. Sometimes police operate under "house rules" that allow them manipulation of the law to their advantage. Inevitably, this leads to not all citizens being given equal consideration when it comes to their right not to be searched. Too often, this happens because of biases—of race, gender, socioeconomic status, location, and so on.

It is from this perspective that Latoya Peterson and Cherisse Santa Cruz Datu's *Contempt* approaches the Fourth Amendment. What *will* it take to bring equity for everyone?

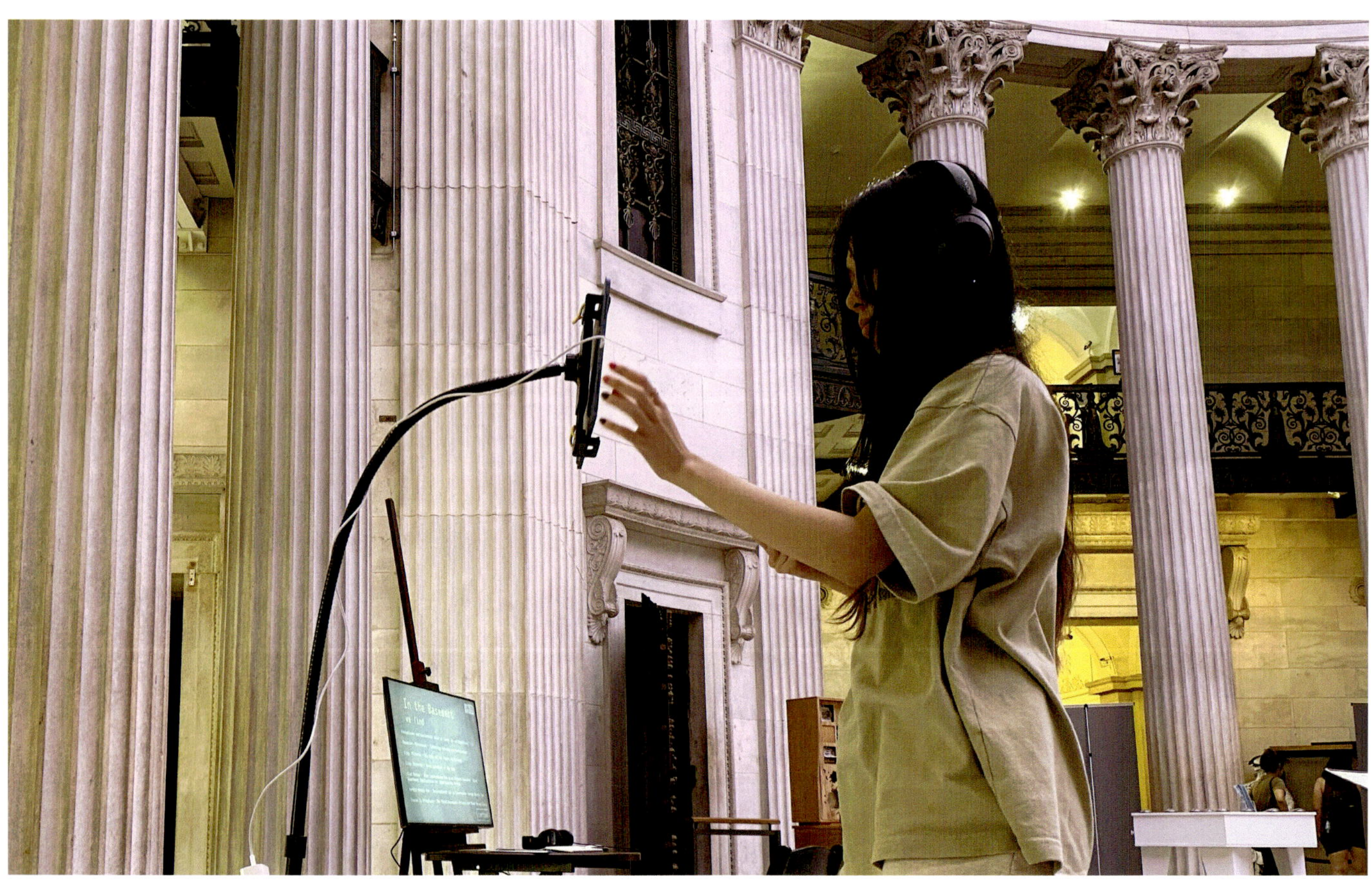

THE FIFTH AMENDMENT

No person shall be held to answer for a capital, or otherwise infamous crime, unless on a presentment or indictment of a Grand Jury, except in cases arising in the land or naval forces, or in the Militia, when in actual service in time of War or public danger; nor shall any person be subject for the same offence to be twice put in jeopardy of life or limb; nor shall be compelled in any criminal case to be a witness against himself, nor be deprived of life, liberty, or property, without due process of law; nor shall private property be taken for public use, without just compensation.

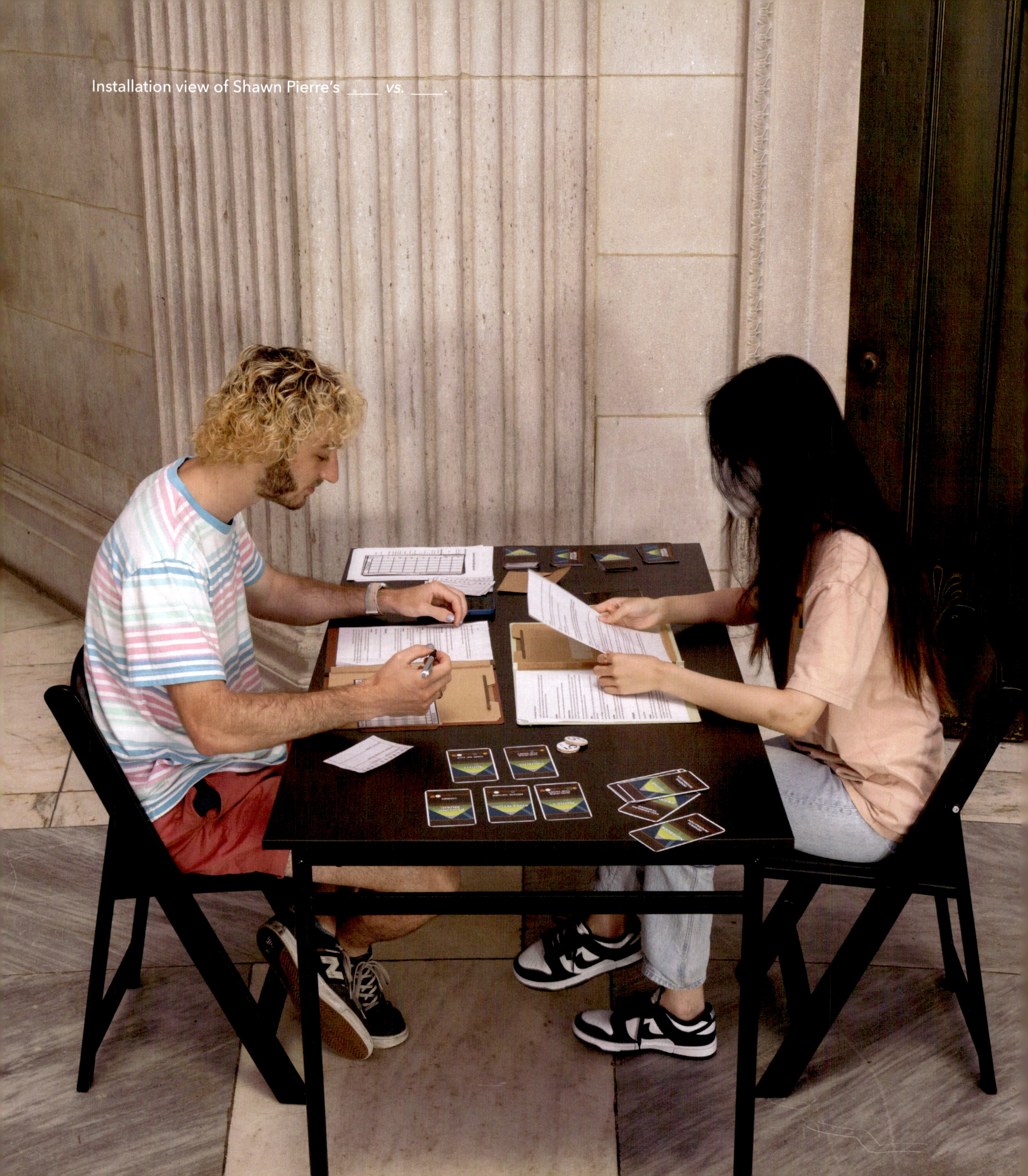
Installation view of Shawn Pierre's ____ vs. ____.

Shawn Pierre

____ *vs.* ____, 2022

Tables, chairs, custom game-card decks, game
   tokens, 4 game folders, writing materials,
   papers, paper clips, overhead lighting
Dimensions variable

> **The Fifth Amendment is a national treasure and an enduring conundrum.**

INTERROGATING THE FIFTH AMENDMENT

MONICA C. BELL
Professor of Law, Yale University

At their best, the Fifth Amendment's five clauses keep the government from railroading people by prosecuting them repeatedly for the same offense ("double jeopardy") and by ensuring that the government cannot prosecute a person unless a large group of the accused's peers agree that the criminal charges are valid ("grand jury"). It intends to ensure that individuals cannot be coerced into testifying against themselves in criminal proceedings ("self-incrimination"). It places limits on how the government can take a person's property ("takings"). It also guarantees "due process of law," which includes more than procedure. Due process of law is capacious; it guarantees a baseline of equality under the law. The Fifth Amendment also protects an array of fundamental rights—the right to privacy, the freedom to marry, and the right to make choices about one's own sex life and reproductive activity. The Fifth Amendment thus touches most aspects of every major domain of public life.

This short essay focuses on the criminal-procedure portions of the Fifth Amendment. The double-jeopardy, self-incrimination, grand-jury, and due-process provisions *together* reveal a fundamental constitutional ethos of limited governmental power to prosecute and punish individuals. Yet ethos and practice never consistently align.

Consider that a substantial number of criminal cases—in some jurisdictions, nearly or more than 90 percent—are resolved through plea bargains. In a plea-bargain process, the prosecutor offers a defendant a reduced sentence for claiming to be guilty and thus not completing a trial. Many plea-bargain processes ensue before a grand jury would hear and validate the charges against the defendant. In a system of plea bargains rather than trials, provisions like the grand jury offer

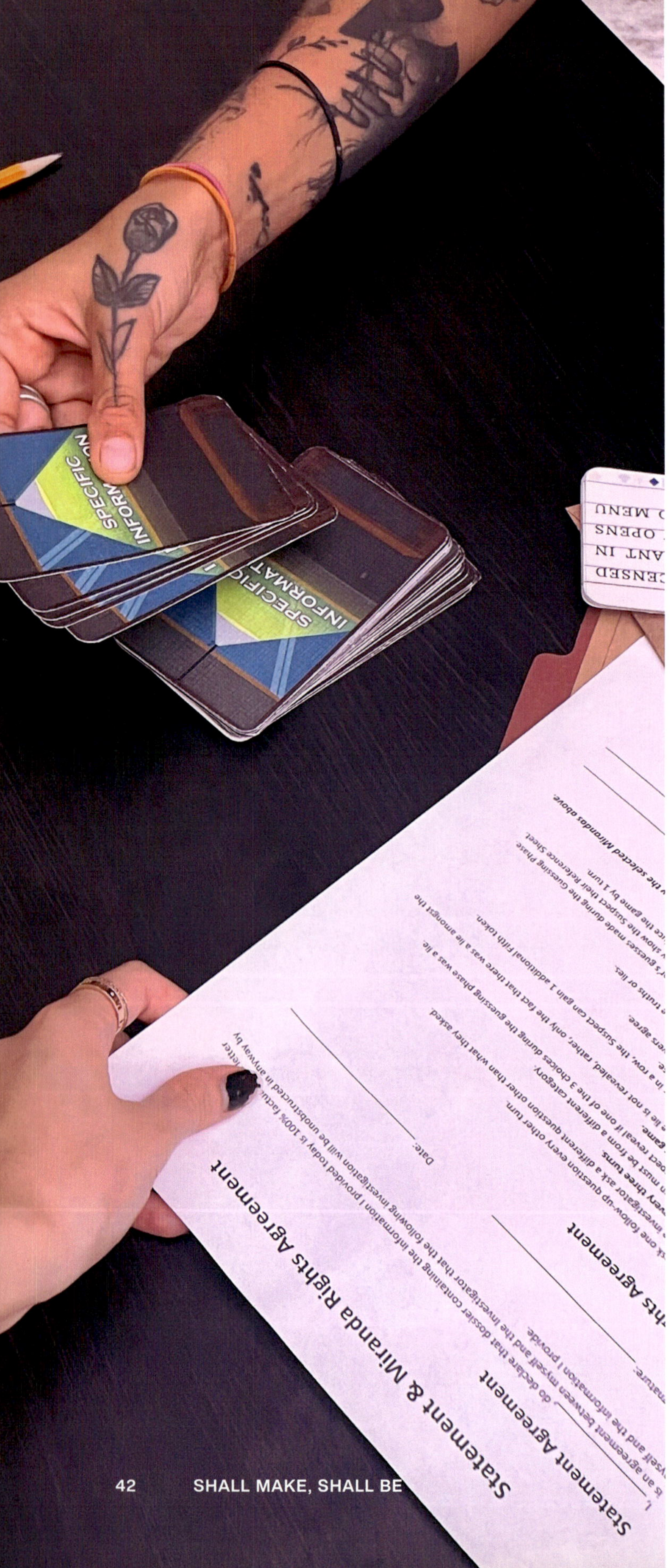

little direct protection. Moreover, analysis of grand juries suggests that they are, on the whole, functionally irrelevant to the modern criminal-justice process, even when cases reach that stage. Prosecutors carefully control the information that grand-jury members receive. For that and other reasons, it is rare that grand juries check prosecutorial power.

The Fifth Amendment protection against double jeopardy is powerful but limited, in several ways. First, our legal systems do not consider "jeopardy" to have started until a deep stage in the criminal case—after the jury has been sworn in, or after a judge has called the first witness in a judge-run (bench) trial. Yet, largely because of plea bargains, most cases do not reach either jury trial or bench trial. When a criminal trial ends in a mistrial, depending on the circumstances, defendants can be retried for the same offense without any violation of the double-jeopardy clause. The double-jeopardy clause does nothing to prevent two different governments (for example, a state government and the US federal government) from prosecuting a person for the same offense at different times. Under US Supreme Court jurisprudence, reaffirmed in 2019's *Gamble v. United States*, the state government and the federal government are "separate sovereigns"—two distinct governments that may separately prosecute an individual for the same offense. Finally, defendants can also receive both criminal punishment and civil liability for the same offense. So, although the state may only try a defendant once for a specific crime, victims' families can sue a defendant for damages to address any injuries that a defendant inflicted. Prosecutors often assist with these layered criminal and civil suits. In all of these ways, the realities of our criminal-punishment regimes in the United States often fail to match up with the spirit of the Fifth Amendment's criminal-procedure provisions—the idea that the government should face very high barriers to restricting individuals' liberties through punishment.

When ethos and reality do align, they do so most robustly for the prominent and the powerful. The June

2021 release of comedian and serial sexual-abuser Bill Cosby from prison after his botched prosecution for sexual assault elicited public aggravation over the Fifth Amendment's "technicalities." After serving three years, Cosby was released because of the misconduct of the prosecutor in his case, who promised that he wouldn't prosecute Cosby if Cosby testified in a civil case. Yet the prosecutor used Cosby's testimony in that civil case—which Cosby only agreed to give once he was assured there would be no subsequent criminal proceedings—against Cosby in criminal court, leading to his conviction. The Pennsylvania Supreme Court overturned Cosby's guilty verdict on the grounds that the prosecutor's actions violated Cosby's due-process and self-incrimination rights under the Fifth Amendment. Some advocates against sexual violence have lamented the final outcome of Cosby's case, arguing that the state's botched treatment of Cosby's case has retraumatized his many victims and sends the message to other survivors that they cannot find justice. To some members of the public, the Fifth Amendment's criminal-procedure provisions, in all of their value, can have frustrating implications for accountability and healing.

These provisions are powerful at times, as the Cosby case illustrates. They join with the Fourth and Sixth Amendments to set a constitutional tone that would on balance empower individual defendants to resist undue efforts to prosecute them. Yet, as important as these protections are, they are an insufficient power-balancing mechanism for most members of marginalized communities who come into contact with harsh, omnipresent, and presumptuous systems of punishment. Cosby was able to hire and fund a team of attorneys who vigorously sought to free him from prison because his Fifth Amendment rights had been violated. However, for a wide swath of Americans—especially those who are both low income and racially marginalized, lacking the wealth and access of Bill Cosby—those protections are not in practice strong enough to guard against systemic bias and keep them out of prison. The sociological realities of the criminal system demonstrate that the Fifth Amendment does not do enough to shield Latinx, Black, and Indigenous poor people from the largely unfettered power of prosecutors while it grants protection to some others.

The Fifth Amendment is a national treasure and an enduring conundrum. It is awesome in its expansiveness, and its criminal-procedure provisions suggest that our nation's systems of punishment may not treat individuals coercively or abusively. Its provisions, and sometimes their impact, are worthy of celebration. Nonetheless, its gaps and vulnerabilities impede its promise as a protector of individuals' rights before the state. Its provisions should be read not as achievements but as promises that demand steady labor toward perfection.

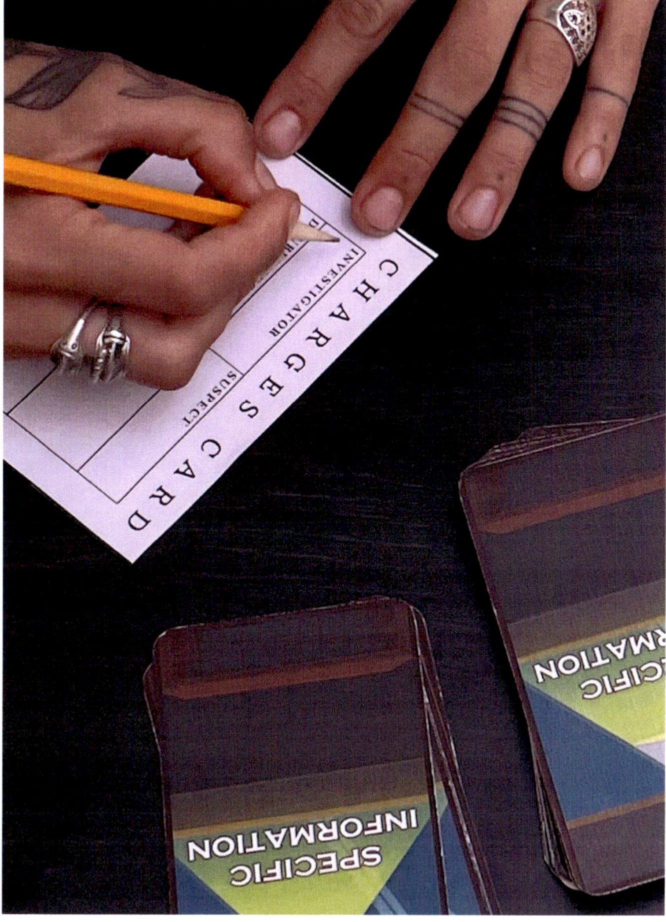

____ vs. ____

____ *vs.* ____ is a verbal deduction game for two players, one Suspect and one Investigator, each with their own goals. For the Investigator to win, they need to figure out which crime the Suspect committed, while the Suspect is trying to trick the Investigator into picking a crime they cannot be convicted of due to the Double Jeopardy Clause. To begin, the Suspect pulls cards from the Crime Deck without showing the Investigator and chooses two crimes—one to be the Committed Crime and one to be the Double Jeopardy Crime—then writes them down and encloses them in an envelope. Following this, the Suspect and the Investigator pull from a variety of other decks that determine what topics can be discussed during the questioning and what information the Suspect can provide.

After all players agree on a list of rules from the Miranda Rights document, the Investigator questions the Suspect in hopes of deducing the crime, while the Suspect chooses when to tell the truth or when to lie with the hope of tricking the Investigator into selecting the wrong crime.

Have I used the Fifth Amendment? Yes, but never correctly, and never in any sort of actual legal situation. Normally, I used it when I refused to admit to friends that I did something I shouldn't have. Everyone knew that I was avoiding telling the truth. It was just a fun thing to say, unless you were on the receiving end of whatever action I was denying.

These feelings of smug joy when playfully declining to share information and of frustration when someone does not admit to something are emotions

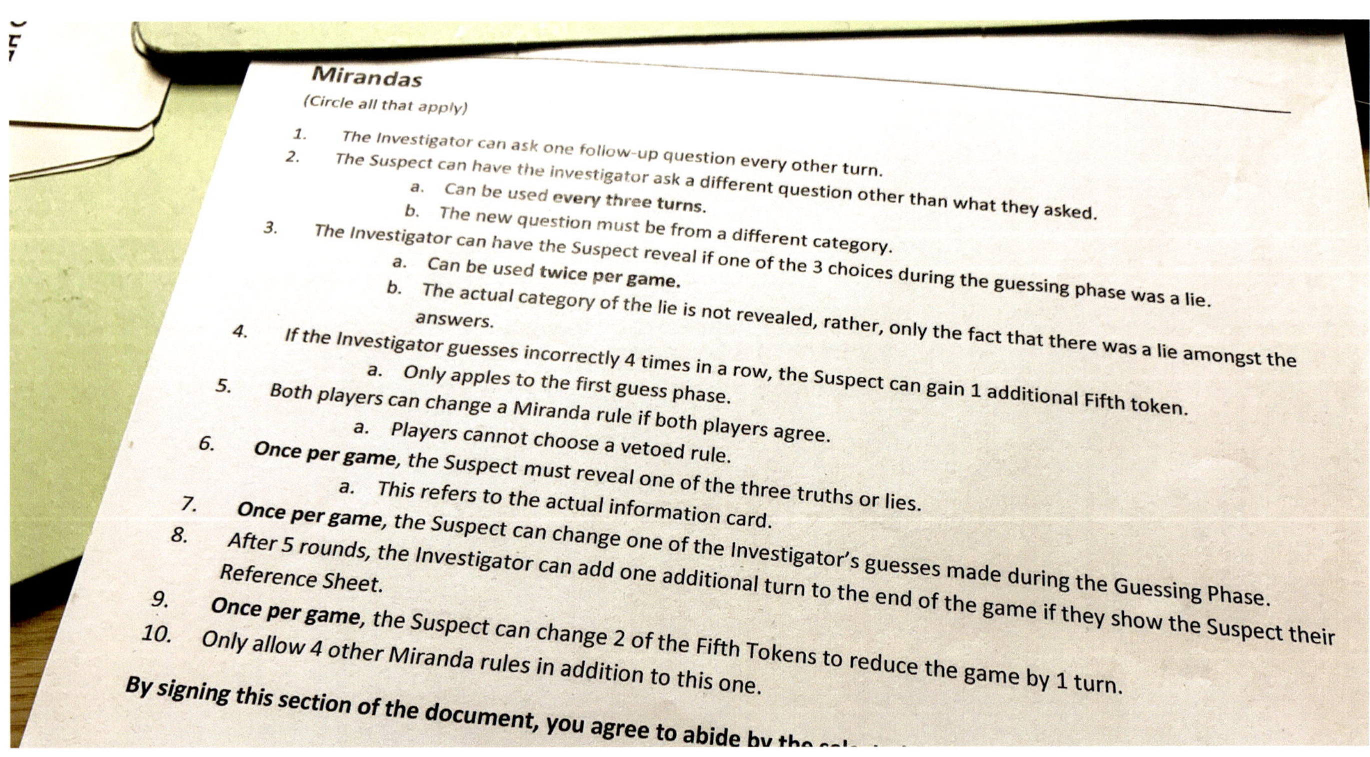

that I want to capture with ____ *vs.* ____ (read as "blank versus blank"). One person is trying their hardest to find out the truth, and the other person is trying their best to frustrate and mislead. The situation is only intensified when the people involved in this interaction know each other. ____ *vs.* ____ plays off these feelings: the hopes of finding the truth, the fear of being found out, and the suspense of getting closer and closer to the end of the game without knowing who has the advantage.

____ *vs.* ____ plays off a few pieces of the Fifth Amendment—more specifically, the Miranda warnings, double jeopardy, and the self-incrimination clause. At the beginning of the game, players agree on the Miranda Rights document, rules, and rights they can enact to help their play or hinder their opponent. During the game, the Suspect can "Plead the Fifth Amendment" when they feel the Investigator is getting too close to solving the crime they committed. Finally, the Investigator must do their best to make sure they do not pick the crime that the Suspect was already tried for. If the Investigator does pick the wrong crime, the Suspect wins due to the Double Jeopardy Clause.

It is understandably tricky to balance a game that asks players to mislead their opponents using information they create on the fly. Much of this relies on how confident a person feels and if they can evade the truth or work their way through their opponent's deception. Ultimately, the experience really comes to life when playing with someone you know well, as players will make assumptions based on information that isn't present. Rather than avoiding that feeling, a feeling that people would fall into naturally, I found that the game was successful when I leaned into those emotions. These emotions help make the interactions between the Suspect and the Investigator unique, something that can't be duplicated but can be understood by others who have participated in the game.

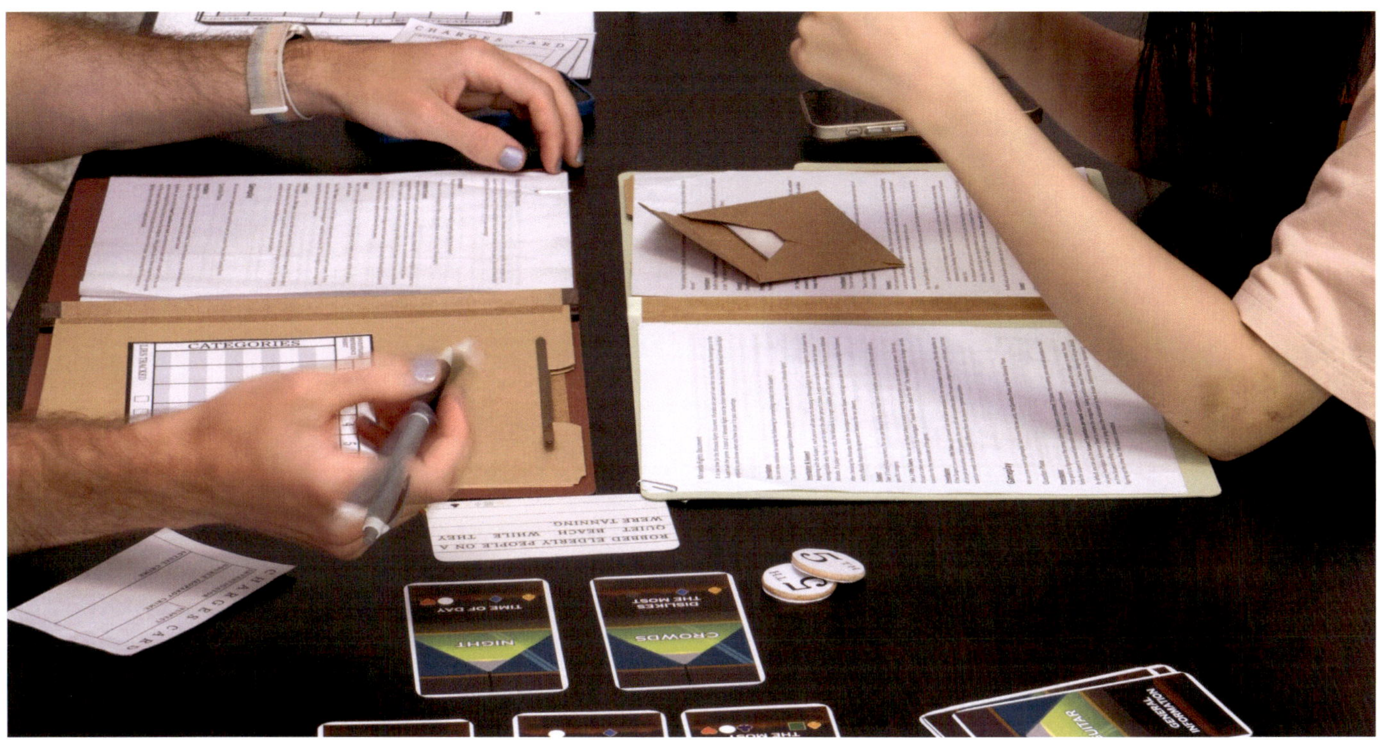

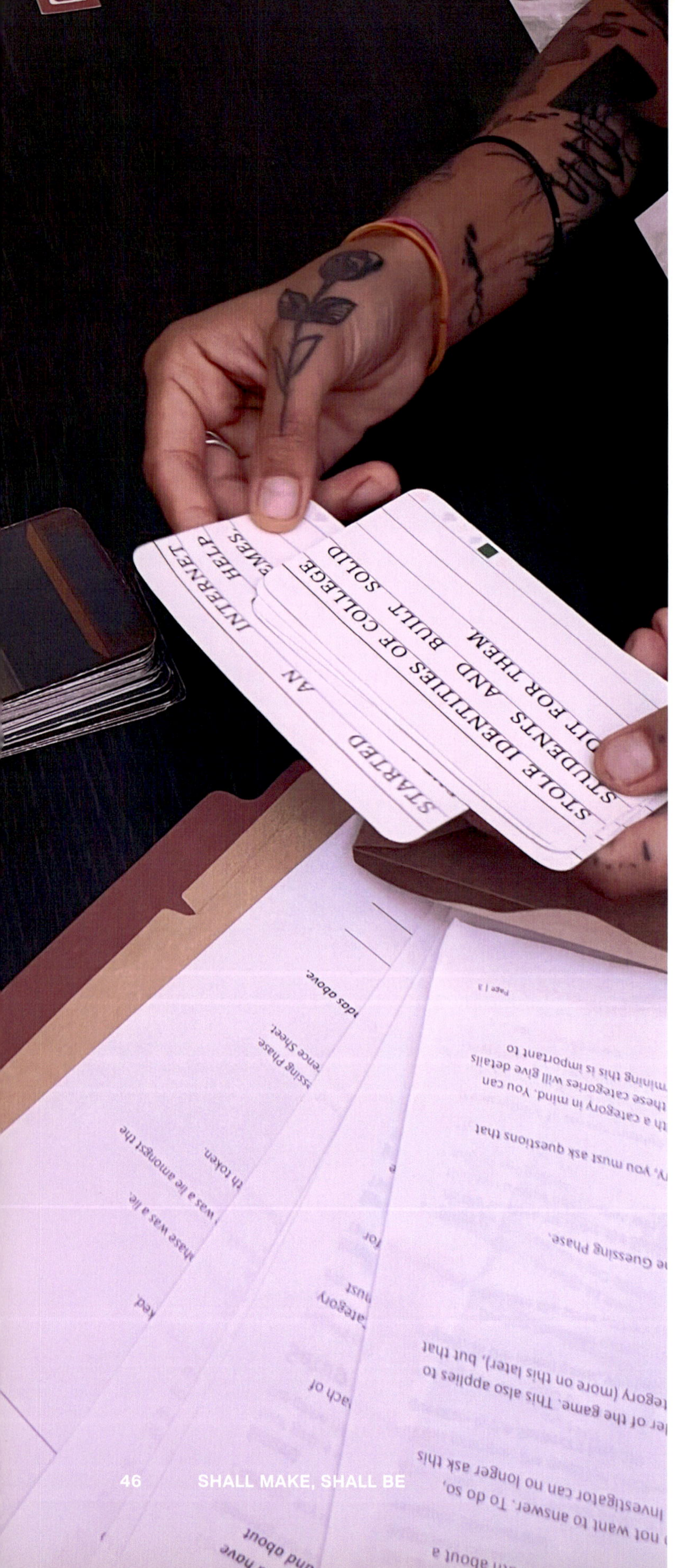

CURATOR COMMENTARY

Viewed from the lens of game design, the third clause of the Fifth Amendment—the source of the right against self-incrimination—appears to be a special-case rule to patch over a loophole in the overarching principles of truthful testimony under oath and the presumption of innocence until proven guilty—if the accused can be compelled under oath to implicate themself, how can they be guaranteed the presumption of innocence? This patch, however, led to an exploit: "On the advice of counsel, I invoke my Fifth Amendment right against self-incrimination." Pleading the Fifth has been viewed as within the letter of the law yet also outside the spirit of fair play within the careful constructs of the US court system. It is a cultural shorthand for the divide between those privileged enough to obtain top-shelf legal support and everyone else.

The Fifth Amendment finds a second life outside the courts—as an often playful, "wink, wink, nudge, nudge" nondenial of something one doesn't want to own up to. It is from this perspective that Shawn Pierre approaches the Fifth Amendment in _____ vs. _____. Emerging from the popular social deduction game genre, Pierre's game surfaces the tensions inherent in pleading the Fifth—one's guilt is presumed but not outright stated. Social deduction games ask players to work together to accomplish a goal while also trying to figure out who among them is working against the group. In _____ vs. _____ , one player attempts to get the truth from the other without the suspect invoking the Fifth.

Pierre's game recontextualizes the playful embodiment of the Fifth Amendment in a light narrative context: that of a simple interrogation room complete with a plain table, sturdy (but not so comfortable) chairs, folders containing paperwork, and, of course, that signature bright light. Consider it a simple set on which the cat-and-mouse game of interrogation and (maybe?) confession unfolds.

THE SIXTH AMENDMENT

In all criminal prosecutions, the accused shall enjoy the right to a speedy and public trial, by an impartial jury of the State and district wherein the crime shall have been committed, which district shall have been previously ascertained by law, and to be informed of the nature and cause of the accusation; to be confronted with the witnesses against him; to have compulsory process for obtaining witnesses in his favor, and to have the Assistance of Counsel for his defence.

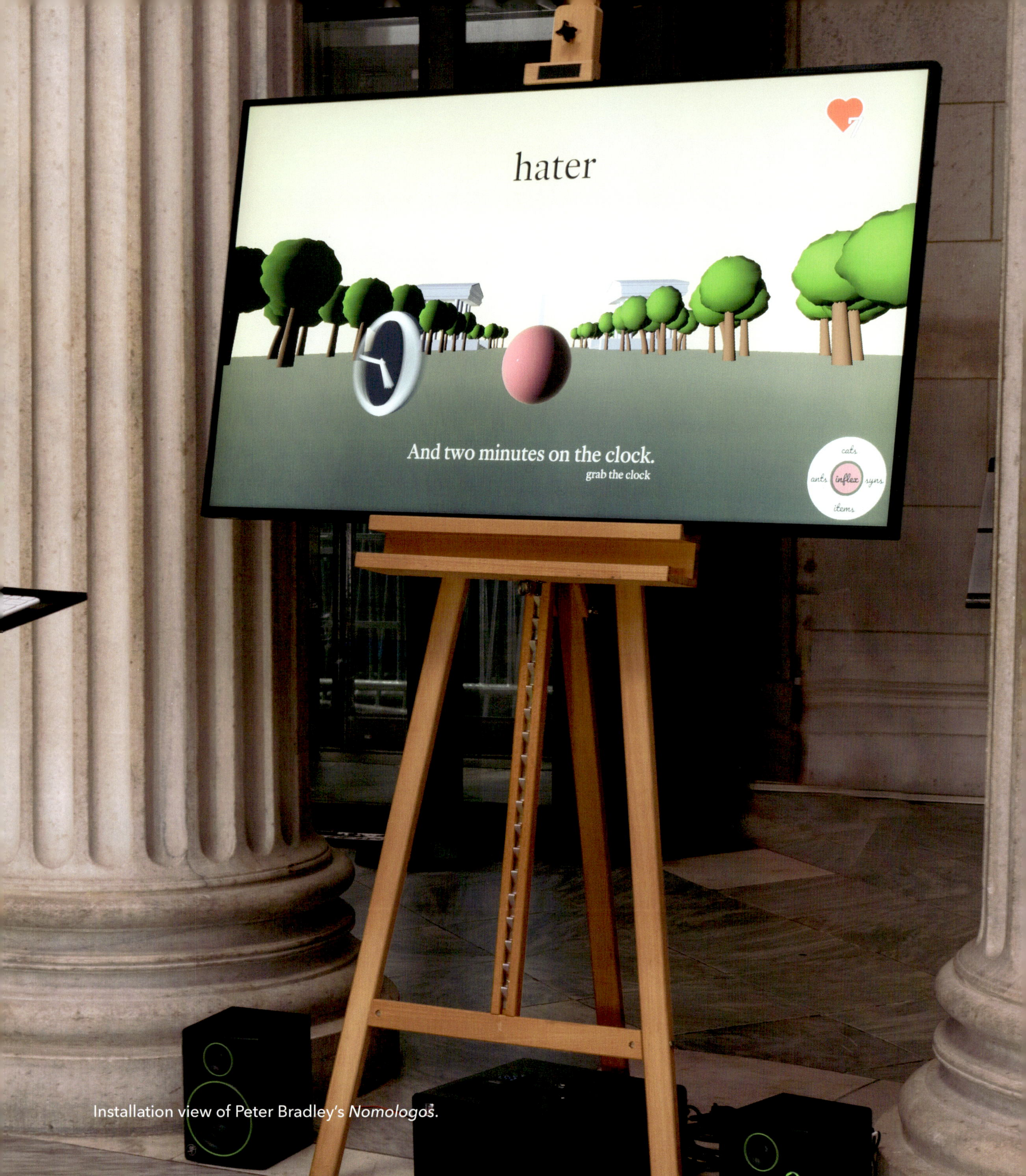

Installation view of Peter Bradley's *Nomologos*.

Peter Bradley
Nomologos, 2022
Computer software with high-
definition video and sound
4 feet by 8 feet

INTERROGATING THE SIXTH AMENDMENT

SUJA A. THOMAS
Professor of Law, University of Illinois

The right to a jury trial was so important to our democracy that when we declared our independence from England, we proclaimed they had "depriv[ed] us in many cases, of the benefits of Trial by Jury." We subsequently set forth the power of juries to decide and the right to a trial by jury in Article III, Section 2 of the Constitution and in the Sixth Amendment in the Bill of Rights.

Despite this constitutional right to a jury trial, the vast majority of people who are accused of crimes do not go to trial. They plead guilty.

Why would anyone plead guilty? They do so for a variety of reasons. One primary reason has to do with a government procedure called the "trial penalty." The government can penalize a person who is accused of a crime who insists on a trial by jury. If a jury finds them guilty, that person is given much more time in prison compared to a person who simply agrees to plead guilty. This penalty for taking the jury trial has contributed to the astonishing statistic that over 95 percent of people who are accused of crimes plead guilty.

Despite the government's prevalent use of plea bargains to incentivize people accused of crimes to plead guilty, this practice was not used at the time of the country's founding. At this earlier time, when the accused were not penalized for taking the jury trial, they would rarely plead guilty. Instead, they would be tried by juries, which often acquitted them.

In a controversial decision in the 1970s, the United States Supreme Court approved of the trial penalty. In that case, a man named Hayes was accused of forging a check for under ninety dollars. The prosecutor told Hayes he would be sent to prison for five years if he pleaded guilty, but he would be sent to prison for life if he insisted on a trial by jury and was convicted. Hayes refused to plead guilty, and after the judge sentenced Hayes to life in prison following this conviction by a jury, Hayes protested that he should not be penalized for insisting on a trial by jury. This violated his constitutional rights. Four justices agreed with Hayes. However, the deciding majority of five justices said his rights were not violated. They emphasized that the "plea bargain [was] an important component of this country's criminal justice system."

The increased use of plea bargaining over time has resulted in juries trying less than 4 percent of criminal cases. Most of the people accused of committing crimes are "convicted" of crimes without people from the community deciding that they have committed the crimes. Instead, one person, often one white, male prosecutor, decides who goes to prison. This fact has contributed to the mass incarceration of people of color, including a disproportionate number of Black people.

How important is the right to a jury trial in today's society? If you are accused of a crime by the government, whom do you want to decide your fate? Do you want the government to decide? Probably not. It has already accused you of a crime. You likely would want the impartial group of people from the community that the Sixth Amendment guarantees—who do not have a bias toward the government.

While no system, including trial by jury, is perfect, many people would choose to have such a group unanimously decide whether they committed a crime versus one prosecutor from the government who has already accused them of the crime.

Moreover, without a trial, the accused cannot confront their accuser, another right guaranteed in the Sixth Amendment. This can result in innocent people being convicted of crimes. Of the people who have been found innocent, 18 percent pleaded guilty—some of whom pleaded guilty due to the trial penalty.

There can be a value to the jury trial separate from findings of innocence. The government may enact unjust laws or may prosecute for reasons that the community finds unjustifiable. The police may go after certain people whom they do not favor. In these circumstances, the jury can nullify or find against the law. This has

happened, for example, in some states where marijuana is illegal and people are prosecuted for growing it for their own or others' use.

There also can be value in the community itself coming together on a regular basis and deciding important issues such as who should go to prison.

How did the right to a jury trial become the right to plead guilty? Presently, in the United States, more actions are illegal than ever before at the same time that additional resources have not been placed in the system. Moreover, the government has every reason to threaten a defendant with more time in prison if they do not plead guilty. The government wins without having to prove anything.

In summary, the right to a jury trial in the United States practically does not exist because defendants would be penalized for exercising the right.

Increased public awareness of this unwarranted penalty and its consequences is necessary to bring back the invaluable right to a jury trial.

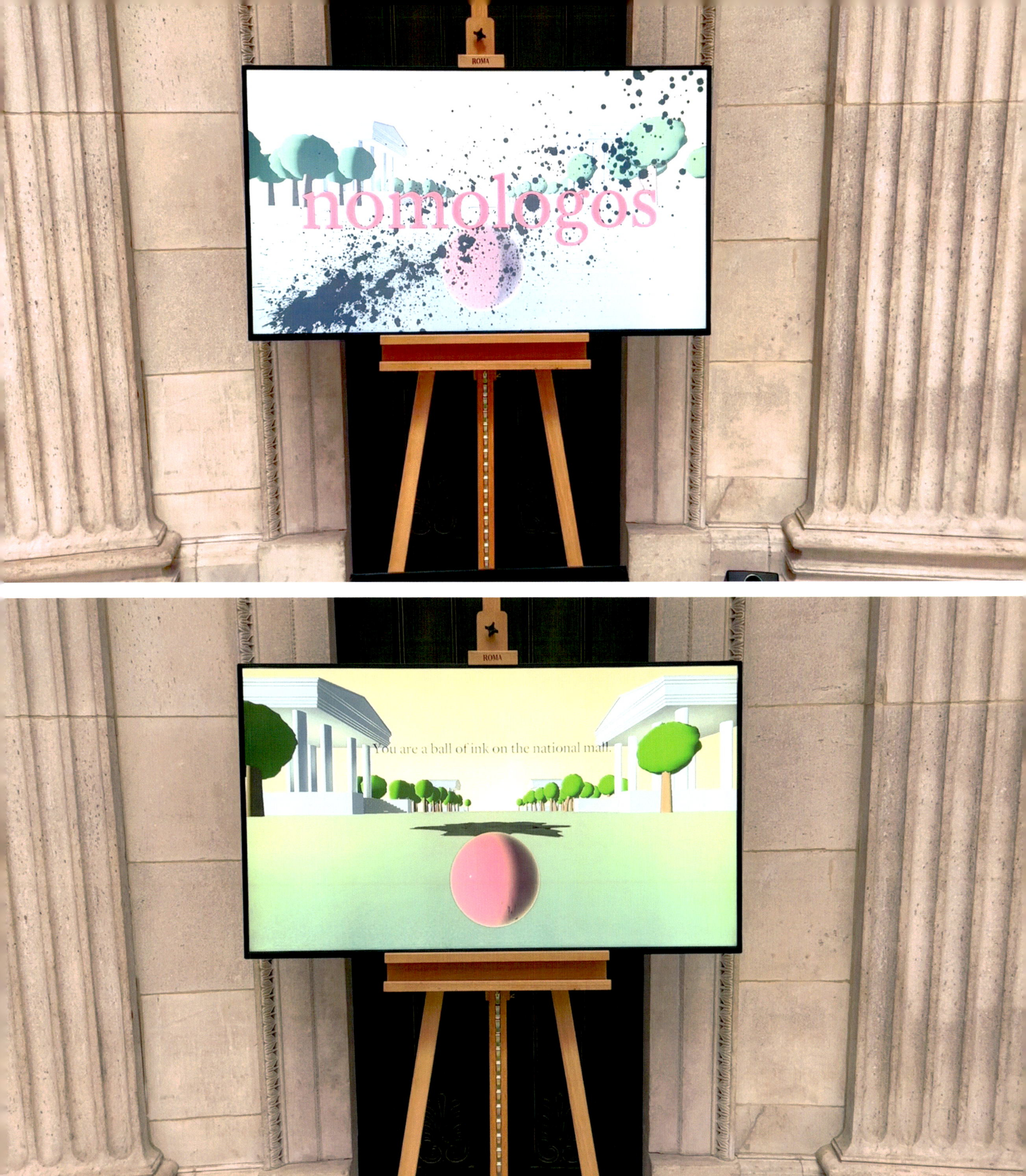
nomologos
You are a ball of ink on the national mall.

ARTIST COMMENTARY

Peter Bradley
Nomologos

Nomologos is a single-player video game about language and the law. It looks like an obstacle course, staged at the National Mall, which the player, acting as a ball of ink, is invited to complete. It differs from a traditional obstacle course in that movement is inferred from a sequence of words, provided by the player via keyboard input. A sequence of synonyms moves right, a sequence of antonyms left. Hypernyms jump; hyponyms duck. An unrelated sequence costs a life, of which the player has a limited supply on their way to the finish line.

Moving between signifiers in this way, the game is meant to be a meditation on the inherent flux of the law. Reflexively, we think of the law as something absolute and inviolable, made from moral truth, prepared by the careful work of reason. In reality, however, the law is made of language, that most yielding of materials, a thin membrane, oscillating in the play of powers. Our understanding of the Bill of Rights and all the liberties it protects is conditioned by the very structure of language, by the way that meaning is made and fixed.

Traditionally, we think of the dictionary as the repository of meaning, and, indeed, the definition of a word gives you something to hold on to on the way to understanding, but definitions are intrinsically superficial. A definition is like a picture of a house. It doesn't consider the plumbing and the electric, the communication of rooms. It is not lived in, from the inside.

From the inside, language is more like a thesaurus. It's a dynamic system of relations: of similitude and difference, of inclusion and exclusion, of echoes morphological and historic. A word acquires meaning against the differential net of all the others, and it keeps its meaning fixed covalently with its neighbors. Words are like a man who is one person at work and another at home and restored to a former self entirely in the company of his childhood friends.

Linguists call these little verbal societies clusters, and in their association the coherence of meaning is sustained. *Nomologos* is an invitation to explore their bonds and boundaries. It is a puzzle whose solution demands a kind of semantic algebra. Across the sequence of signifiers that comprise the game, the player will encounter the core concepts of the Sixth Amendment—"speedy," "public," "impartial," "vicinage," "notice," "witness," "counsel"—and from these landmarks circumlocute the hermeneutic space of jurisprudence.

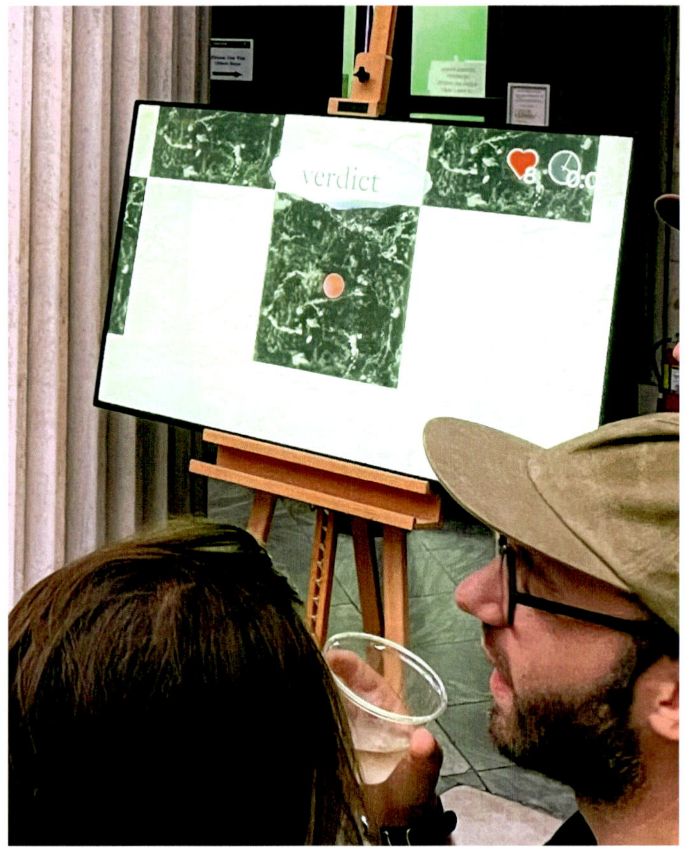

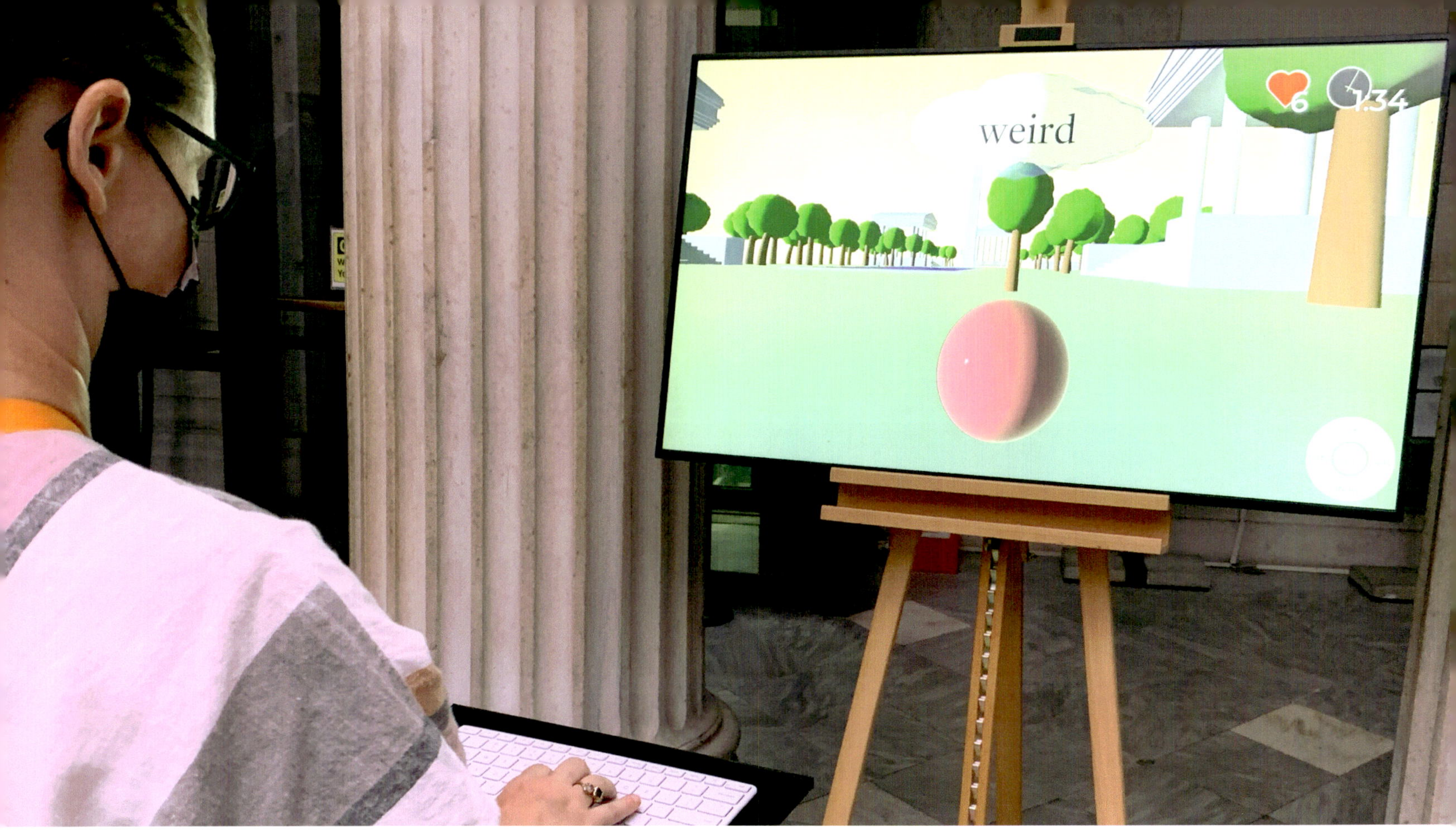

weird
6
1:34

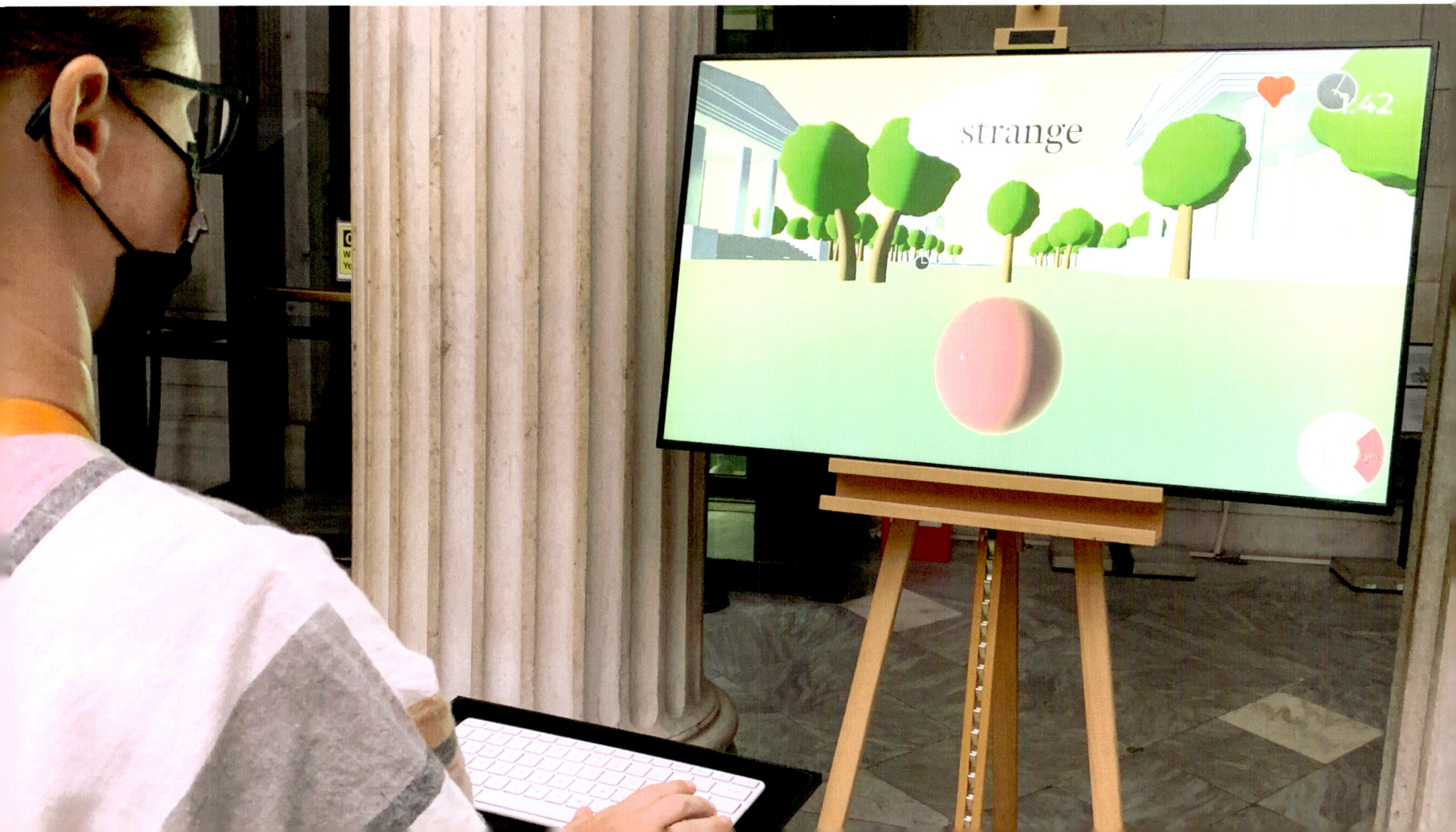

strange
1:42

Words are contingent, even those in which we invest a good deal of trust. Words can be circumvented and otherwise worked around. The Constitution constructs ways of being together from words, leaving us with an infrastructure ripe for use, abuse, and misuse. This plays out in the Sixth Amendment—though not found within the amendment's language, the "trial penalty" Suja A. Thomas discusses sidesteps the intention of the Sixth for the vast majority of those accused of a crime. If the words guaranteeing us the right to a speedy and public trial are put in jeopardy by the threat of greater penalty from that very trial, what value does the Sixth Amendment hold for most accused?

Peter Bradley's *Nomologos* considers an underlying tension of how to interpret the Bill of Rights as a whole and the ways in which the Sixth Amendment is interpreted in particular. We treat the Constitution and the Bill of Rights as "set in stone," despite the changes in context, time, and everything else that has unfolded in the years since 1789. Can we assume the intentions behind the eighty-one words in the Sixth Amendment mean the same thing today they did twenty-three decades ago?

The gameplay of *Nomologos* is similar to that of an "endless runner"–style game: the player moves forward in a three-dimensional space attempting to collect rewards and avoid obstacles. Where it differs is in the control scheme. Rather than using buttons to move left, right, up, and down, the player types words semantically related to the words on screen organized along the sides (for left and right movement) and top and bottom (for jumping or ducking). The layered cognitive load of using language to navigate space proves to be a compelling metaphor for a layperson's attempts to navigate the fraught space of a jury trial.

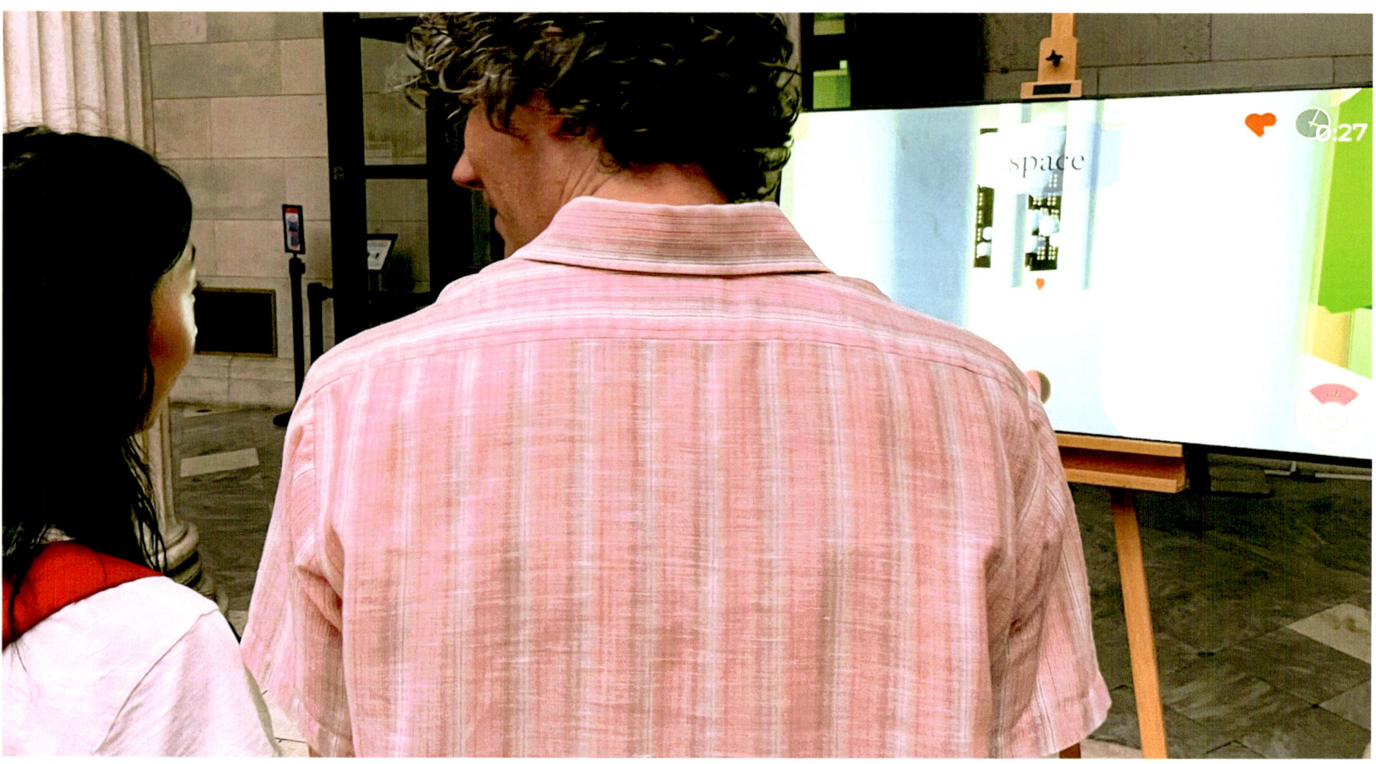

THE SEVENTH AMENDMENT

In Suits at common law, where the value in controversy shall exceed twenty dollars, the right of trial by jury shall be preserved, and no fact tried by a jury, shall be otherwise re-examined in any Court of the United States, than according to the rules of the common law.

Installation view of Arnab Chakravarty, Ian McNeely, and Moaw!'s *Verbal Gymnastics*.

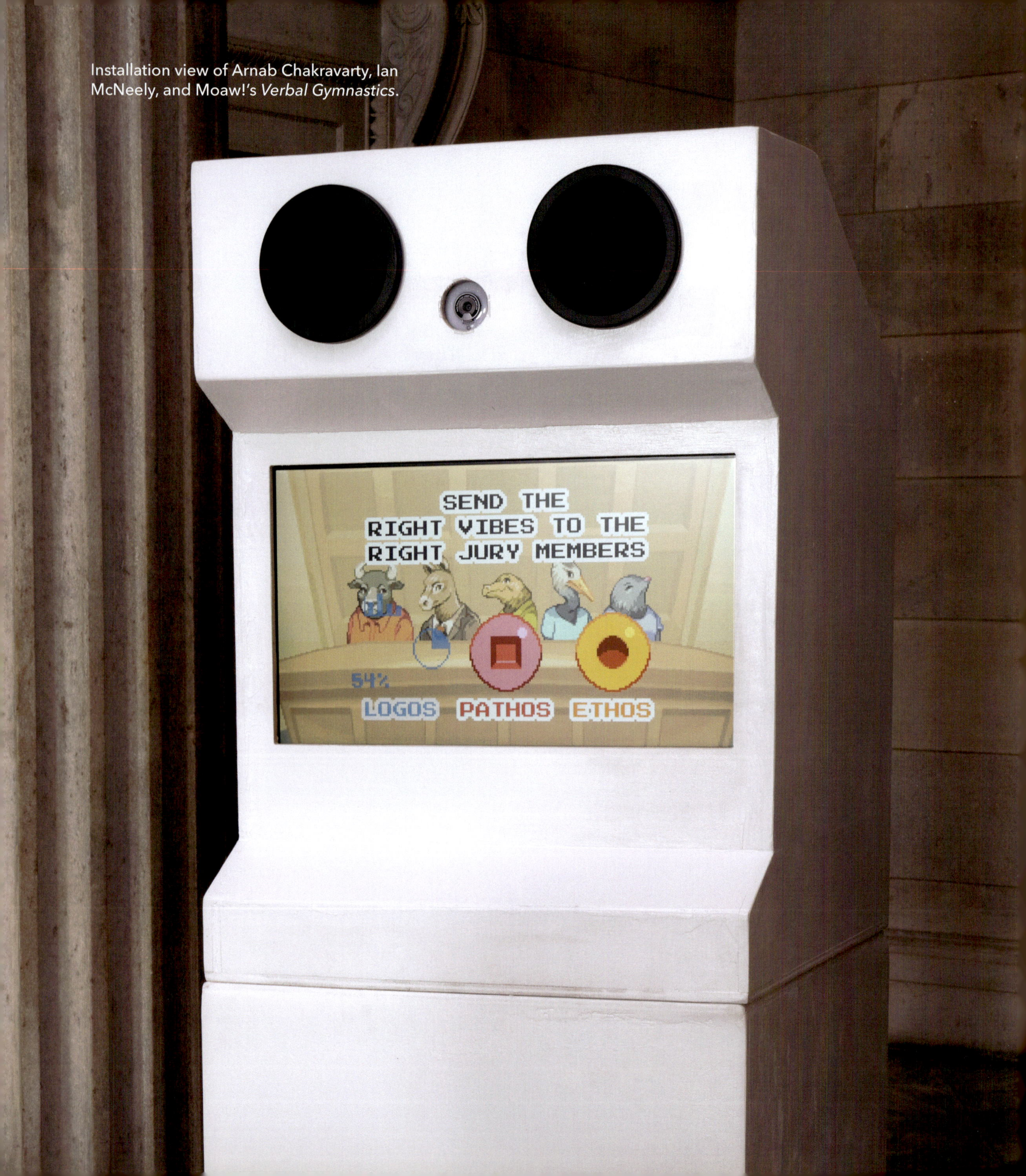

Arnab Chakravarty, Ian McNeely, and Moaw!
Verbal Gymnastics, 2022
Arcade cabinet with a single screen, computer,
    webcam, and sound
Cabinet dimensions: 29.5 inches wide by 29.5 inches
    deep by 78.75 inches high

The Seventh Amendment protects citizens from the abuses of the rich, the powerful, and the well connected.

INTERROGATING THE SEVENTH AMENDMENT

MICHAEL E. SHAMMAS

Forrester Fellow, Tulane University

In 1776, the Declaration of Independence's drafters famously wrote:

The history of the present King of Great Britain is a history of repeated injuries and usurpations, all having in direct object the establishment of an absolute Tyranny over these States. To prove this, let Facts be submitted to a candid world.

Not insignificantly, included among the twenty-seven "Facts . . . submitted to a candid world" was that King George III had "depriv[ed] us in many cases, of the benefits of Trial by Jury."

After ratifying the Constitution, which went into effect on March 4, 1789, the right to trial by jury was considered so crucial that it was detailed in the document at least three times: first, in Article III, Section 2; second, in the Sixth Amendment, which guarantees the right to trial by jury in federal criminal cases; and, finally, in the Seventh Amendment, which guarantees the right to a trial by jury in federal civil cases "where the value in controversy shall exceed twenty dollars."

The Seventh Amendment is one of the most important but least appreciated constitutional amendments. While the Sixth Amendment's guarantee of a criminal jury protects citizens from overzealous government, the Seventh Amendment's guarantee of a civil jury protects citizens from abuse by other Americans. As William Blackstone noted in 1783, the civil jury "preserves in the hands of the people that share which they ought to have in the administration of public justice, and prevents the encroachments of the more powerful and wealthy citizens." Put more simply, the Seventh Amendment protects citizens from the abuses of the rich, the powerful, and the well connected.

Unfortunately, the Seventh Amendment has more force on paper than it has in reality. This is for several reasons.

First, the capabilities of civil juries, of "We the People," have been questioned—and calls for "tort reform" have increased—because of the misrepresentation of high-profile tort cases. Several reasons underlie this misrepresentation. Although not all of them are malicious, it cannot be denied that many corporations have spent millions of dollars promoting misconceptions about the necessity of "tort reform" to dilute the ability of ordinary Americans to hold them accountable when they commit crimes or otherwise injure citizens.

One such sensationalized case is *Liebeck v. McDonald's Restaurants*, commonly called the "hot-coffee case." As a 2011 documentary (aptly titled *Hot Coffee*) discussed, the case was distorted in popular culture to such an extent that many Americans continue to believe that the elderly victim, who recovered money due to injuries sustained after spilling McDonald's coffee on her lap, suffered only superficial burns. She was actually hospitalized for eight days and needed another two years of medical treatment.

It nonetheless remains popular to deride juries and to demand "tort reform," even though excessive reform in some states, which limits the amount of damages that plaintiffs can recover, have resulted in perverse outcomes. Injured consumers or victims of medical malpractice are now sometimes unable to recover enough money to even pay for their medical bills, because state legislatures responding to corporate lobbyists have passed legislation establishing caps on damages. Consumer advocates like Ralph Nader have understandably called this sort of tort reform "tort *de*form."

Second, and relatedly, it is becoming increasingly difficult to buy any product or participate in any service without "agreeing" to "arbitration." Arbitration is a process by which parties involved in a dispute resolve their differences privately before an arbitrator instead of publicly before a judge. If you look at your credit card agreement, there's a large chance that—simply by using that card—you have "agreed" to arbitrate any dispute.

There is nothing wrong with arbitration *per se*. It can

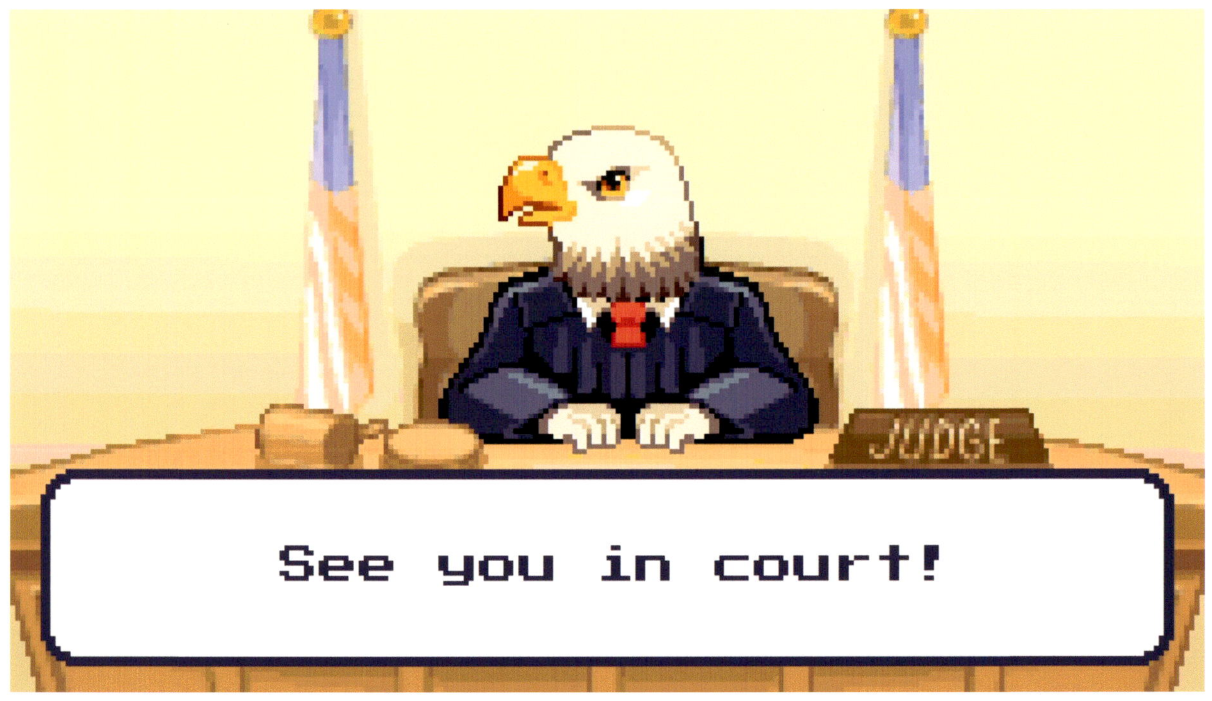

habitually save time and money, and though there is some evidence that arbitrators sometimes favor the interests of corporations over individuals, this is not necessarily the rule. What *is* troubling, however, is the proliferation of *mandatory* arbitration, which has been on the rise and which prevents citizens from going to court when they are harmed by companies, banks, their employers, and others.

Mandatory arbitration received a boost (and the Seventh Amendment received two punches in the gut) at two pivotal moments in the past century. First, Congress passed the Federal Arbitration Act of 1925, which explicitly directs federal courts to enforce arbitration agreements in lieu of civil litigation. Second, in a 5–4 Supreme Court opinion decided in 2011 (*AT&T Mobility LLC v. Concepcion*), the late justice Antonin Scalia authored an opinion that—by allowing corporations to force consumers to proceed in individual private arbitration instead of in court as part of a class—made it much easier for corporations to prevent citizens from invoking their Seventh Amendment right to go to court and to be heard in public and by their fellow citizens or a publicly accountable judge.

In discussing the Sixth Amendment's jury guarantee in criminal trials, Suja A. Thomas wrote in the Sixth Amendment chapter of this book that "[i]f you are accused of a crime by the government, whom do you want to decide your fate? Do you want the government to decide? Probably not." After all, in criminal cases, the government is prosecuting you.

The Seventh Amendment is no less valuable. If you are involved in a dispute with your landlord, your bank, or your employer, whom do you want to decide your fate? Whom do you want to decide whether a corporation's drive for profit caused it to ignore safety concerns? Whom do you want to decide what is and what is not acceptable in our society? A private arbitrator with (likely) a corporate background? Or a group of fellow citizens?

The answer is obvious. By reframing what corporate lobbyists misleadingly call "tort reform" and by punishing corporations who force consumers to sign arbitration agreements that undermine their Seventh Amendment rights, we can begin to reinvigorate one of our Constitution's most effective protections for average citizens: trial by jury.

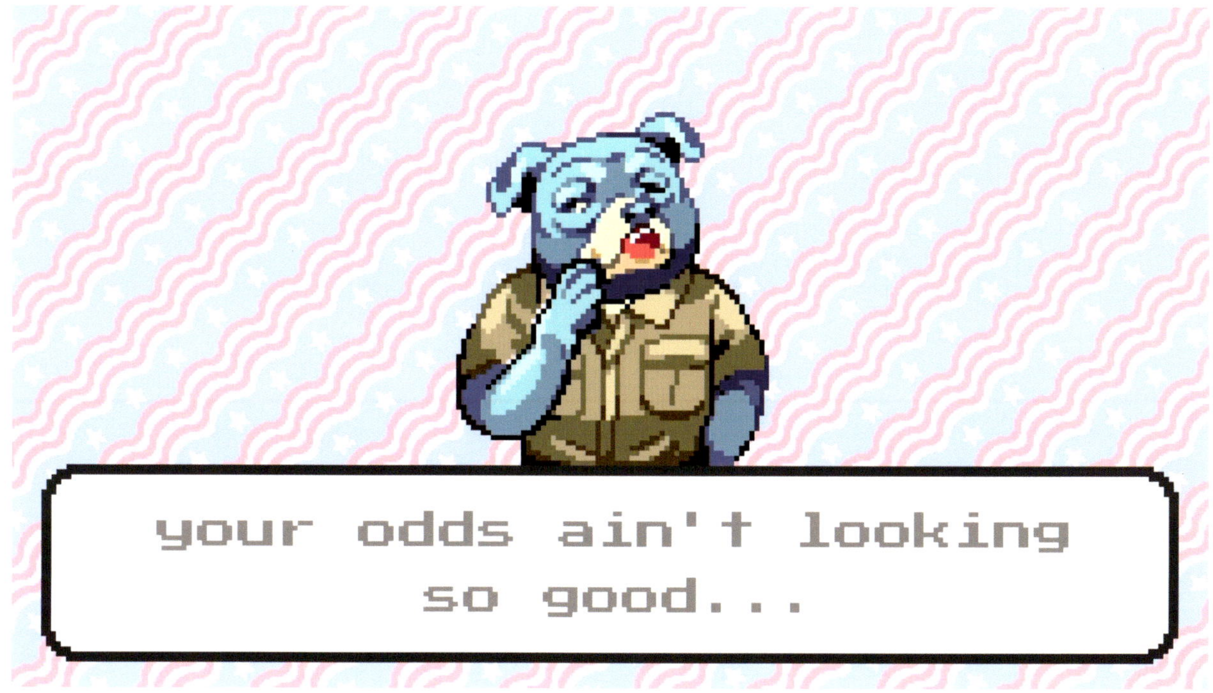

ARTIST COMMENTARY

Arnab Chakravarty, Ian McNeely, and Moaw!
Verbal Gymnastics

Verbal Gymnastics is a single-player, motion-activated arcade game. Built as an arcade cabinet, the game features a gesture-based interface where players' hands are tracked by a camera and projected on the screen. The gameplay draws its inspiration from rhythm games and challenges players to collect colored orbs to impress the five jury members across three rounds. In each round, the game presents the player with five tracks (one track each for each jury member) and a stream of approaching orbs that the players have to use their hands to collect. Each jury member has a preference for and dislike of particular colors, and players avoid catching orbs that jury members dislike on their track. As the players collect the right orbs without catching the incorrect ones, they build up a streak, which increases the impact of their performance on the jury and thereby on the final verdict.

By establishing a constitutional right to a trial by jury, the Seventh Amendment introduces the wildest and most unpredictable of variables into the American civil-justice system: human beings. With *Verbal Gymnastics*, we aimed to create a bespoke arcade game that facilitates the exploration of that human element. Why an arcade game? They're exceptionally inclusive and engaging. Like jury trials, arcade games have a performative component. They are public spectacles that welcome an audience and invoke discussion. They're easy for a casual participant to learn but challenging to master. And the structure of our arcade game is replayable across multiple cases with exciting decisions and varied results. We are daring players to experiment and explore civil-jury trials, seeking new outcomes and pioneering new high scores.

There is also a broader question we hope audiences will examine: "Was justice served?" These

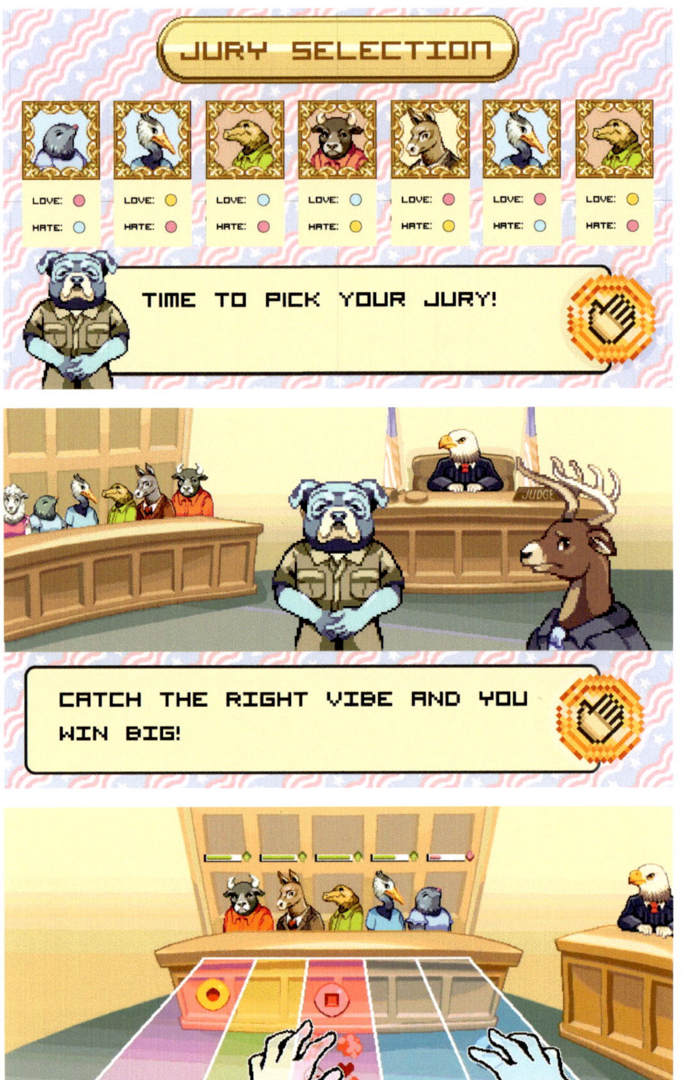

are the words that conclude each game of *Verbal Gymnastics*. They point to the paradoxical nature of a system of law that tasks imperfect people with pursuing a perfect ideal. And since the Seventh Amendment endows ordinary people with the power to award or deny justice, we must cultivate curiosity about justice in ordinary people.

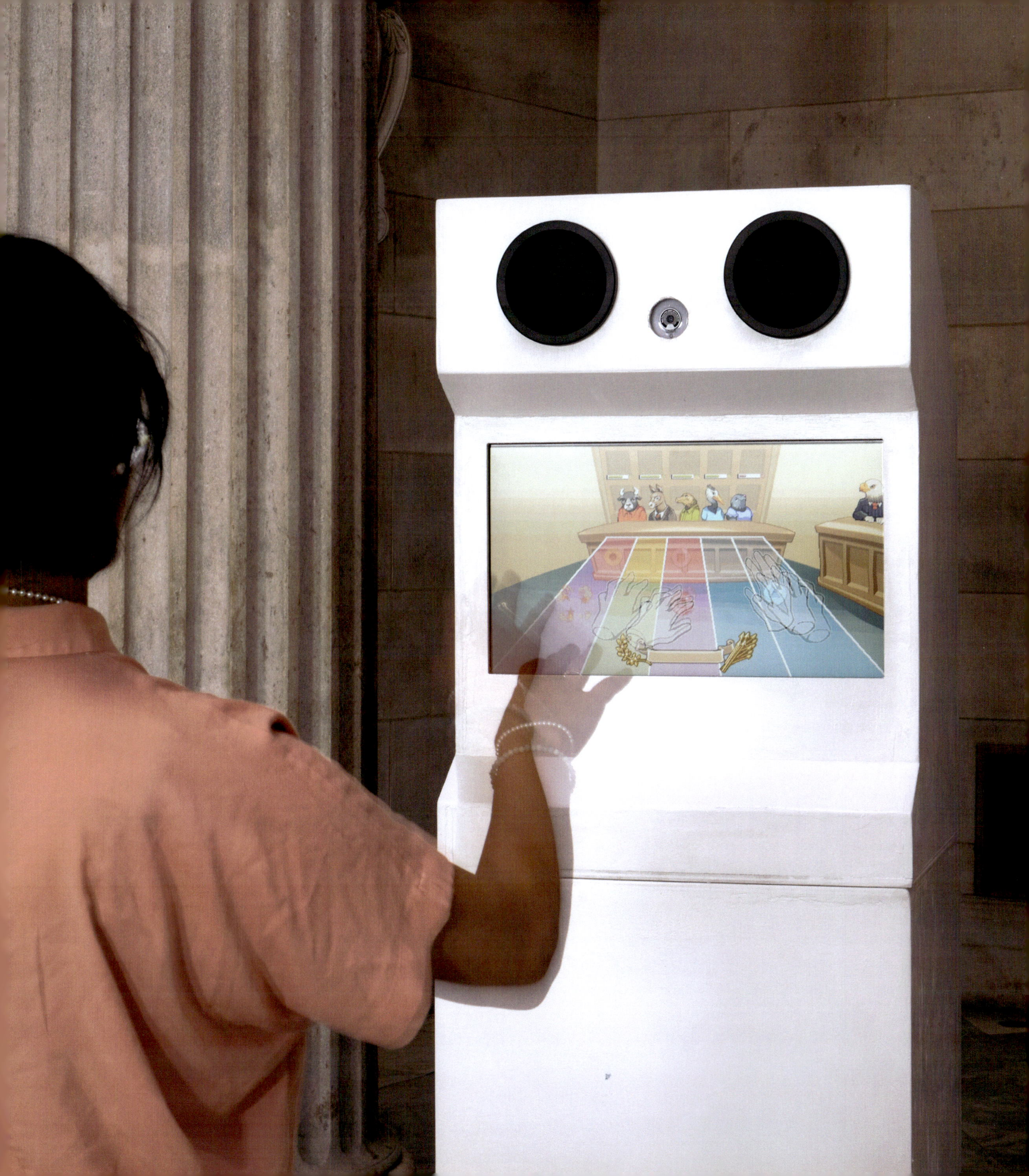

CURATOR COMMENTARY

The Seventh Amendment invests authority in the truth-deciphering skills of a jury. Inside of this is an assumption that a group of individuals can extract truth from the flow of narratives and evidence of the two parties. Though not applied to states, the social form of the jury trial—one not elaborated upon in any detail within the amendment's fifty words beyond the hand-waving toward whatever might be implied as "common law"—became sacrosanct in court trials. The stakes are high for a jury's ability to perform this duty. How does one ensure that a jury will indeed locate the truth and pass down the appropriate verdict?

Using the play idiom of Bemani games—otherwise known as rhythm games, like *Dance Dance Revolution* or *Rock Band*—*Verbal Gymnastics* poses these questions as a playable reflection on what passes muster with a jury. The work explores two questions: What if a jury based its decisions on gestures rather than words? Would expectations of fact, truth, innocence, and guilt change?

Players find themselves having to perform their innocence for a jury of creatures. Dressed quite regally, perhaps in a nod to the interpretation of "common law" based on seventeenth-century English law, the *Verbal Gymnastics* jurors bring with them the idiosyncrasies one might expect from a jury. Players enact their innocence before the jury by performing a series of requested hand gestures. Jurors then interpret the player's truthfulness and pass judgment accordingly.

Despite its cute characters and disarming play, the game mirrors the real challenges of putting one's fate into the hands of a jury. If the decision of a jury is absolute—something debated but not overturned—how do we ensure a jury makes equitable and fair decisions? Why do we believe the "magic circle" of a court proceeding invests jurors with truth-telling powers that override their biases and beliefs? For those studying games, the phrase "magic circle" holds special meaning. Derived from the medieval historian and moralizing theorist Johan Huizinga's *Homo Ludens: A Study of the Play-Element in Culture*, the phrase speaks to the situations in which people determine to abide by customs that may not apply to other moments of our lives. The magic circle was only one of a number of situations Huizinga notes as locations where "special rules obtain": tennis courts, temples, stages, card tables, and courts of justice. From this list, game designers, theorists, and scholars homed in on the magic circle as the stand-in for the ways in which people adopt different values and rules inside of certain situations and contexts. Huizinga recognized the imperative of those with important roles inside a court of justice to behave differently, to set aside the daily, and to accept their place in "temporary worlds within the ordinary world, dedicated to the performance of an act apart."

In the case of a jury, this act apart is impartial evaluation of a case. But as game scholars and theorists have noted, there is no clean departure from the ordinary world. We can't set aside who we are and how we are in order to carry out an "act apart."

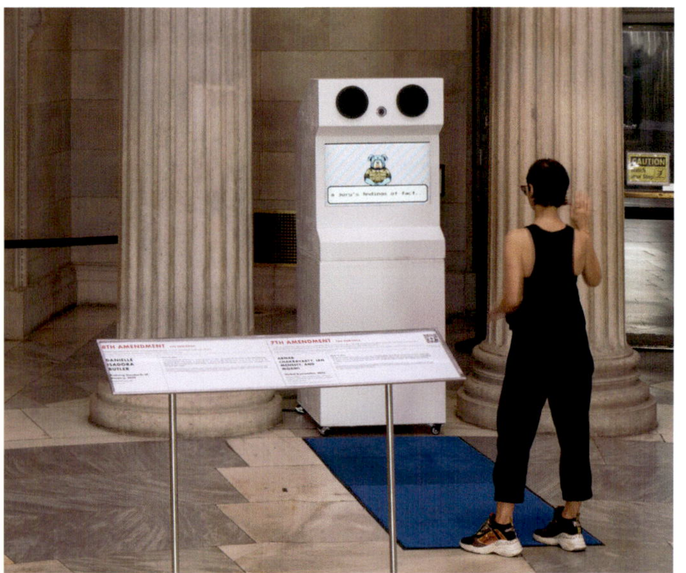

THE EIGHTH AMENDMENT

Excessive bail shall not be required, nor excessive fines imposed, nor cruel and un-usual punishments inflicted.

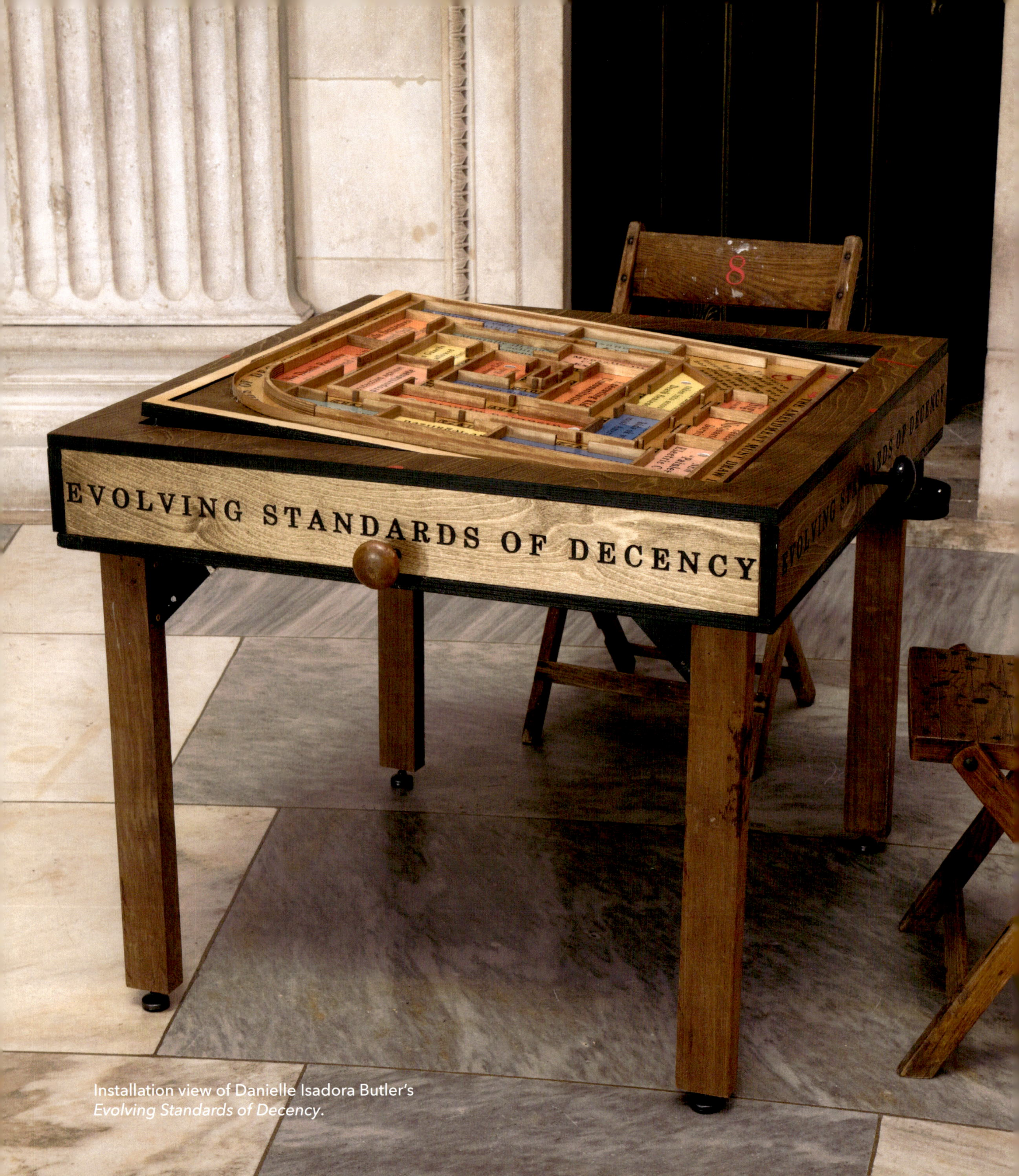

Installation view of Danielle Isadora Butler's
Evolving Standards of Decency.

Danielle Isadora Butler
Evolving Standards of Decency, 2022
Gimbaled maze
30-inch by 30-inch table with chairs

INTERROGATING THE EIGHTH AMENDMENT

KERAMET REITER
Professor of Criminology, Law & Society,
School of Law, University of California, Irvine

Twelve score and five years after the "founding fathers" crafted the succinct text of the Eighth Amendment, everything about punishment in America is excessive.

The Eighth Amendment to the US Constitution is the tersest of the first ten constitutional amendments. Sixteen words prohibit three categories of legal sanctions: excessive bail, excessive fines, and cruel and unusual punishments. However simple, the amendment's agenda remains unrealized.

The prohibitions on excessive bail and fines are minimally enforced. The Supreme Court only just ruled—in 2019—that the Eighth Amendment prohibition on excessive fines applies to state governments.[13] Yet twelve score and five years after the "founding fathers" crafted the succinct text of the Eighth Amendment, everything about punishment in America is excessive: 2.3 million people incarcerated (including thousands in decades-long solitary confinement), 7 million people under correctional control, and 73.5 million people with criminal records of arrest or conviction. The United States bears the highest incarceration rate in the world—twice Russia's rate, and five times higher than China's.[14]

Such excess often overwhelms efforts to establish "unusualness," except in the most egregious cases. Since 1990, only 7 of the 195 countries in the world have executed people who were children (under eighteen) at the time of their crimes. One in eight of these executions (nineteen total) took place in the United States.[15]

---

13. *Timbs v. Indiana*, 586 U.S. ___ (2019).
14. For statistics about US incarceration and criminal-justice-system contact, see https://www.prisonpolicy.org/global/appendix _countries_2021.html. For statistics comparing US rates to other countries, see https://www.prisonstudies.org.
15. The Death Penalty Information Center provides the most up-to-date statistics on the history and characteristics of US executions, and Amnesty International tracks global executions. For data about juvenile executions and international comparative statistics, see: https://deathpenaltyinfo.org and https://www.amnesty.org/en.

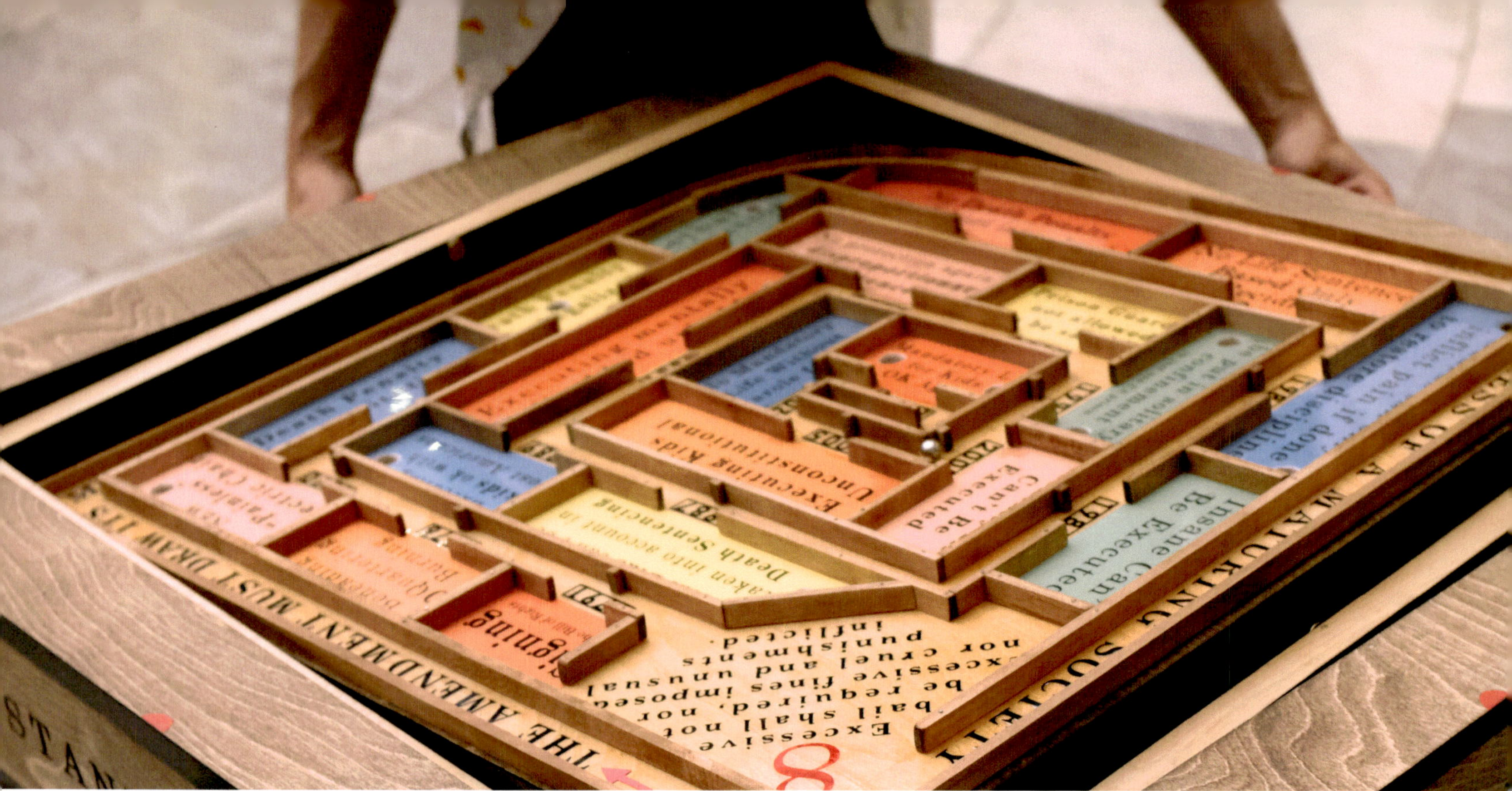

In 2005, the US Supreme Court took note of the global unusualness of this punishment and finally forbade it.[16] Standards of decency had evolved, the Court said. Evolution is a central principle of Eighth Amendment interpretation; as a society evolves, its standards for acceptable punishments evolve, too.[17] Yet kids in the United States can still be sentenced to life without the possibility of parole, often dubbed a de facto death sentence. Standards of decency evolve haltingly—if they evolve at all.

Cruelty is easier to establish—in common sense, if not in law. People charged with crimes can be required to forfeit their possessions, mortgage their property, and even declare bankruptcy to pay their own or their immediate families' bail or punitive fines. People convicted of crimes spend months and years in filthy, overcrowded prison facilities, where violence (individual and structural) is omnipresent and healthcare is scarce. In the 2010s, for instance, the US Supreme Court noted that one prisoner per week was dying "needlessly" because of inadequate medical care in California.[18] In 2020, people in US prisons were five times more likely to get infected with COVID-19 and three times more likely to die than the average US resident. PrisonPandemic, a website archiving the stories of people living through the pandemic in prison, catalogs hundreds of stories, each with a twenty-character-or-less title.[19] The terse titles are as vivid as the Eighth Amendment's terse prohibitions are vague: "Careless Staff." "No Enforcement." "We're Scared." "Kids Suffering." "Coming to Terms." "Dropping Like Flies." "Trouble Breathing." "Hungry Most Days." "Want to Go Home." "Never Ever Imagined."

---

16. *Roper v. Simmons*, 543 U.S. 551 (2005).
17. *Trop v. Dulles*, 356 U.S. 86 (1958).
18. *Brown v. Plata*, 563 U.S. 499 (2011).
19. See https://prisonpandemic.uci.edu.

Our correctional system imposes other de facto death sentences, too. In jails—pre-trial incarceration facilities—suicides are the leading cause of death. Rates of suicide for prisoners in solitary confinement are five times higher than the rates of suicide in the general prison population.[20] Across the United States, tens of thousands of prisoners regularly spend months, if not years, in long-term solitary confinement, in sensory-deprivation conditions known to cause extreme physical and psychological harm. To date, no Eighth Amendment challenge has established any broad limitations on the lengths of time people can spend in solitary confinement. However, the United Nations has determined that as few as fifteen days in solitary confinement might constitute cruel, inhuman, and degrading treatment, if not torture.[21]

In practice, the Eighth Amendment protects the punished from only the most egregiously extreme sanctions—execution, sometimes; gross medical neglect, if enough people die; decades in solitary, maybe. Terse language has enabled slippery working definitions and malleable legal arguments about evolving standards of decency. A seemingly straightforward Civil War–era prohibition has further thwarted the Eighth Amendment's evolution toward decency. In 1865, the Thirteenth Amendment abolished slavery in the United States—"except as punishment." Although slavery ceased to be a legal status permitting commodification of people in the United States, it remains a legally permissible form of punishment.

Like slavery, punishment is racially concentrated. Today, Black people represent 13 percent of the overall US population but 33 percent of America's prisoners, 42 percent of people on death row, and 48 percent of people serving life sentences.[22] A broader system of fines, fees, and post-incarceration collateral consequences, including restrictions on both access to social services and democratic participation, reinforces these racial disparities—weaving a web of "New Jim Crow" regulations.

Day-to-day experiences of incarceration produce the most vivid examples of reenslavement. For instance, in 2002 (137 years after the ratification of the Thirteenth Amendment), the Supreme Court chastised Alabama prison officials for tying Larry Hope to a hitching post, shirtless in the summer sun, without water or bathroom breaks, for seven hours. The brutality was "obvious" to the Court, not least because the hitching post looked so much like a tool of slaveowners.

Still, Hope ultimately lost his claim for damages. He failed to establish *deliberate indifference*—that prison officials had actually known they were causing him harm when they tied him to the hitching post.[23] Establishing deliberate indifference, a requirement courts have read between the few lines of the Eighth Amendment, puts an oppressive burden of proof on victims like Hope, who have few resources (legal, financial, or strategic) with which to prove what a victimizer is thinking. Indeed, the standard subtly shifts legal responsibility for enforcing and protecting rights from the punisher to the punished. In Larry Hope's case, this individualization of responsibility left him with little recourse to either challenge the conditions of his confinement or escape the literal chains in which he was held.

For Hope, for children sentenced to life without parole, for people in prison dying by COVID-19 or suicide, for people in long-term solitary confinement, the Eighth Amendment offers only the slimmest possibility of protection from excess or cruelty. Some people might hope that our criminal-justice system, under the intended restrictions of the Eighth Amendment, could function humanely. Everyday punitive practices continue to prove those people wrong.

---

20. For data about prison and jail suicide rates, see https://www.prisonpolicy.org.
21. See the Nelson Mandela Rules: https://www.unodc.org/documents/justice-and-prison-reform/Nelson_Mandela_Rules-E-ebook.pdf.
22. For data on racial disparities in the criminal justice system, see https://www.prisonpolicy.org.
23. *Hope v. Pelzer*, 536 U.S. 730 (2002).

Danielle Isadora Butler

Evolving Standards of Decency

Evolving Standards of Decency is a gimbaled maze. The maze makes up the top of a table. Players sit on all four sides. A marble is guided by tilting the surface of the maze. Like the classic tilting maze from childhood, this one has barriers to work around and holes to avoid. The path of the maze takes you through the evolution of major Eighth Amendment cases in chronological order. Each case is summarized and simplified in the graphics on the playfield. The 1879 *Wilkerson v. Utah* is distilled into "No beheading, quartering, or burning." The step from there to the case that deemed the electric chair to be humane, instantaneous, and painless is straight—a small step in our evolution. The goal of gameplay is to stay on the path and not fall into the holes. Holes represent the areas of the punitive system that are not protected by the Eighth Amendment or when the Court had "fear of too much justice," as Justice William Brennan put it in the 1987 case that decided that proven racial bias in death-penalty sentencing can't be taken into account. If you can avoid the holes and make it to the center of the maze, the graphics end in 2021.

The American criminal-justice system is overwhelmingly large and dauntingly broken. This piece is made to be approachable. I want you to touch it and interact without instruction. I want its subject matter to be small enough to enable you to ponder this deeply hurtful system while remaining curious. I want us to remember that the things that are considered normal right now might soon be considered abhorrent.

The language of the Eighth Amendment is squidgy. "Excessive" can only be known by comparison to something lesser. What is considered "cruel and unusual" can only be based on an agreed-upon usual. In 1958 (*Trop v. Dulles*), the Supreme Court stated that those open-ended words "draw [their] meaning from the evolving standards of decency that mark the progress of a maturing society." The Eighth Amendment shifts with culture. It is important to remember that culture is malleable and that you make up that culture—that you are partially responsible for that change or lack of change. This piece invites you to navigate the evolution of major Eighth Amendment cases. It highlights how far we have come and how recently it was constitutional to—for example—execute a child. It is easy to imagine that evolution is linear. For four years in the 1970s, the United States didn't allow capital punishment. And despite a fifteen-year trend toward progressive sentencing for children, in 2021 we returned to allowing mandatory life without parole for kids. The curving track of the maze shows that evolution doubles back in labyrinthine loops. Progress toward being less cruel is hardly assured.

The language I use to summarize the cases is chosen to remove the distance that jargon allows. The system as a whole perpetuates because the divides of race and class separate people with privilege and power from communities most impacted. By replacing *juvenile* with *child* and *offender* with *person* in the summary of a case on the gameboard, I hope to subtly bring us closer to remembering the humanity of people in prison. And that if you have never had your family or community torn apart through incarceration, you should know that the biggest difference between juvenile offender and naughty child is most likely the work of privilege.

Like the pathway of this maze, the legal scope of the Eighth Amendment is narrow. Through what is on and off the "playing field," I want us to consider what and who gets left out of the legal protection offered by the Eighth Amendment. The amendment does not extend

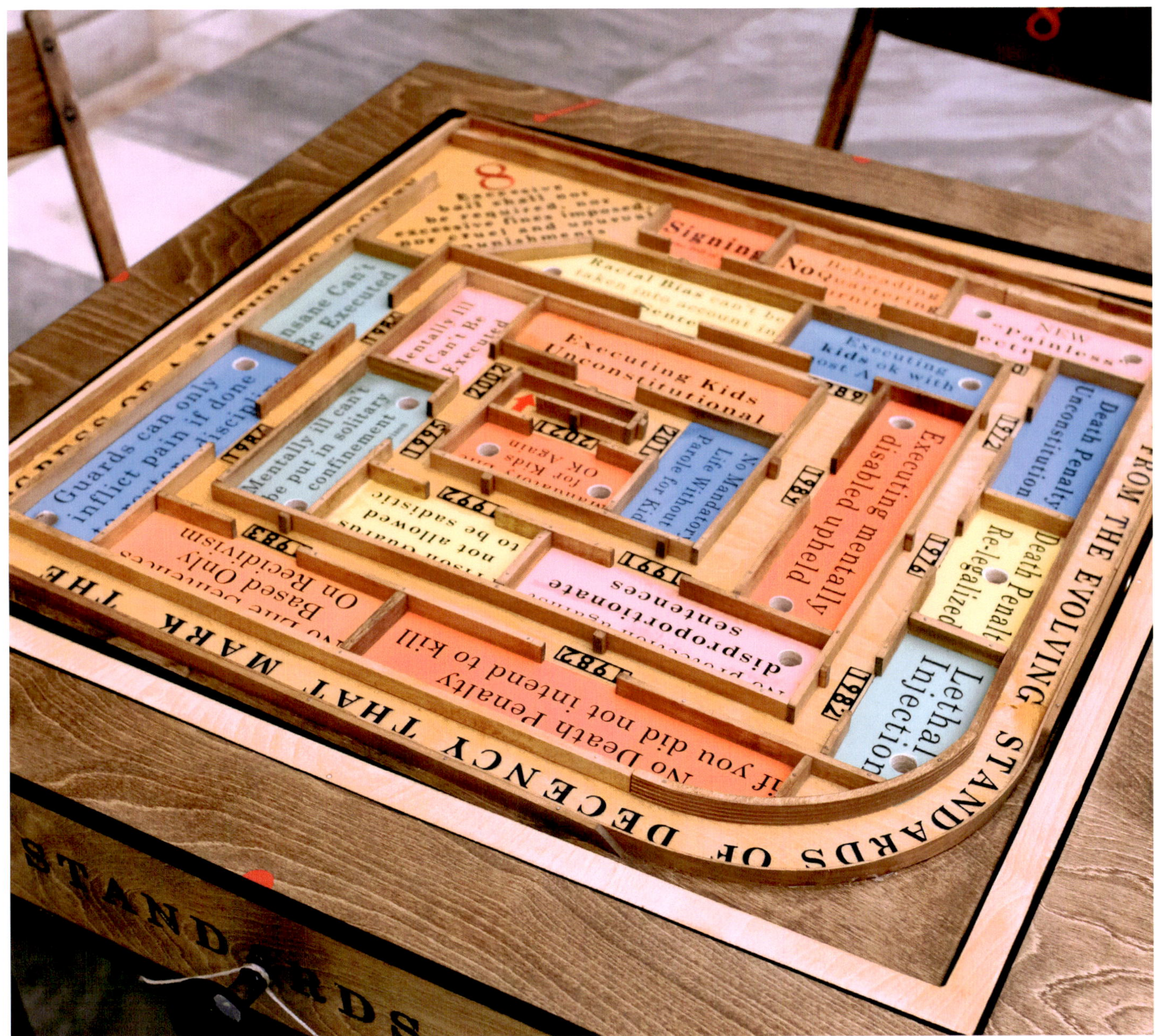

to people in immigration jail, the amendment doesn't protect people on Rikers Island awaiting sentencing, and most cases concerning prison conditions don't make it to trial. In sentencing a judge gives years, yet statistically they are also likely sentencing a person to sexual assault, violence, and a drop in life expectancy.

Through the simple action of a gimbaled marble maze, I hope to juxtapose the promise of the Eighth Amendment with our evolution thus far.

I would like to thank Robin Reid, Olwyn Conway, Keramet Reiter, Paul Grotas, Lea Rosen, Marty Tankleff, Marc M. Howard, Sara Bennett, and Alec Karakatsanis for generously sharing their expertise.

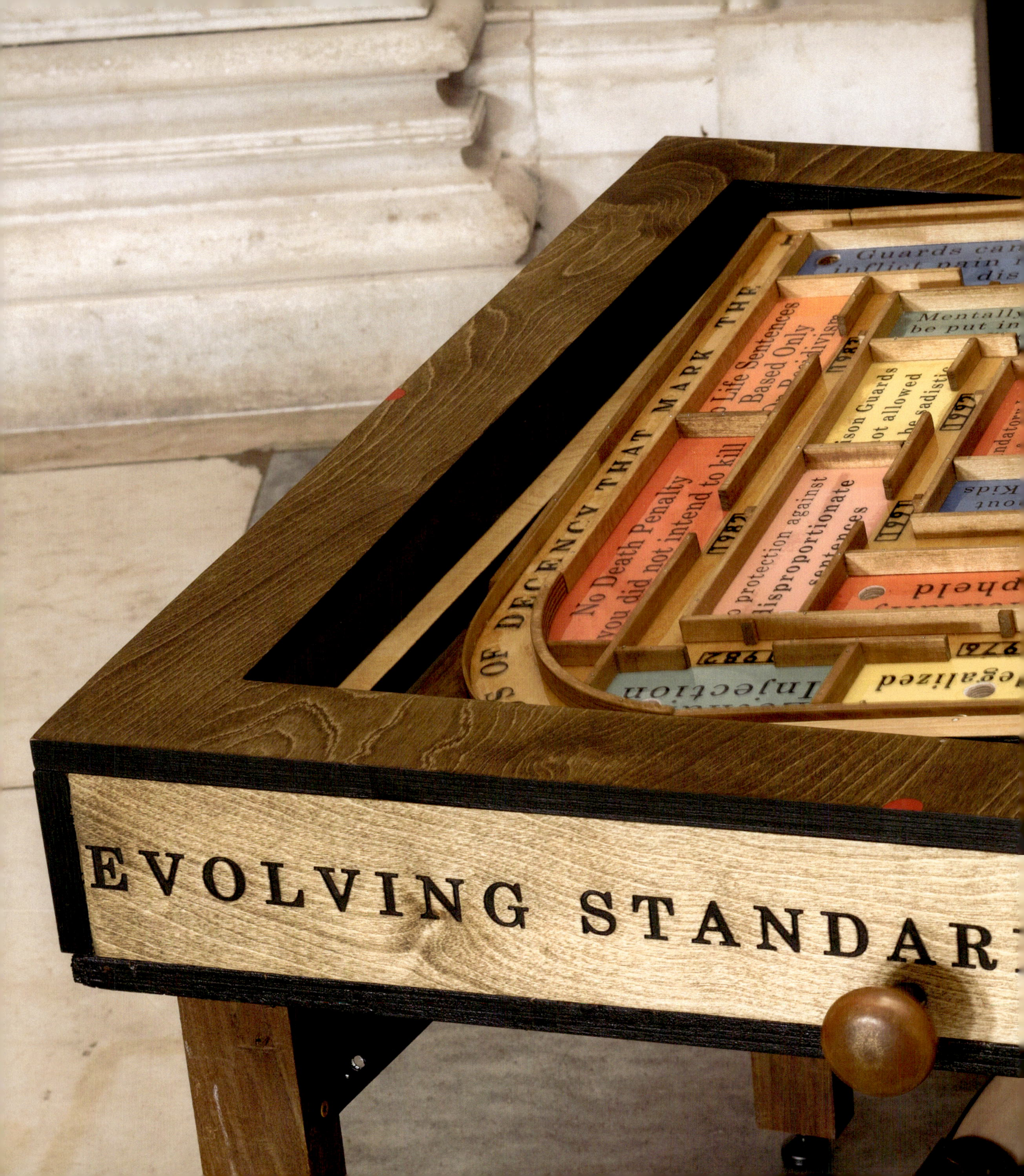

EVOLVING STANDAR
S OF DECENCY THAT MARK THE
No Life Sentences
Based Only
No Death Penalty
you did not intend to kill
Guards can
inflict pain
dis
Mentally
be put in
Prison Guards
ot allowed
the sadistic
protection against
isproportionate
sentences
Injection
egalized
pheld
1982
1987
197
1976
199

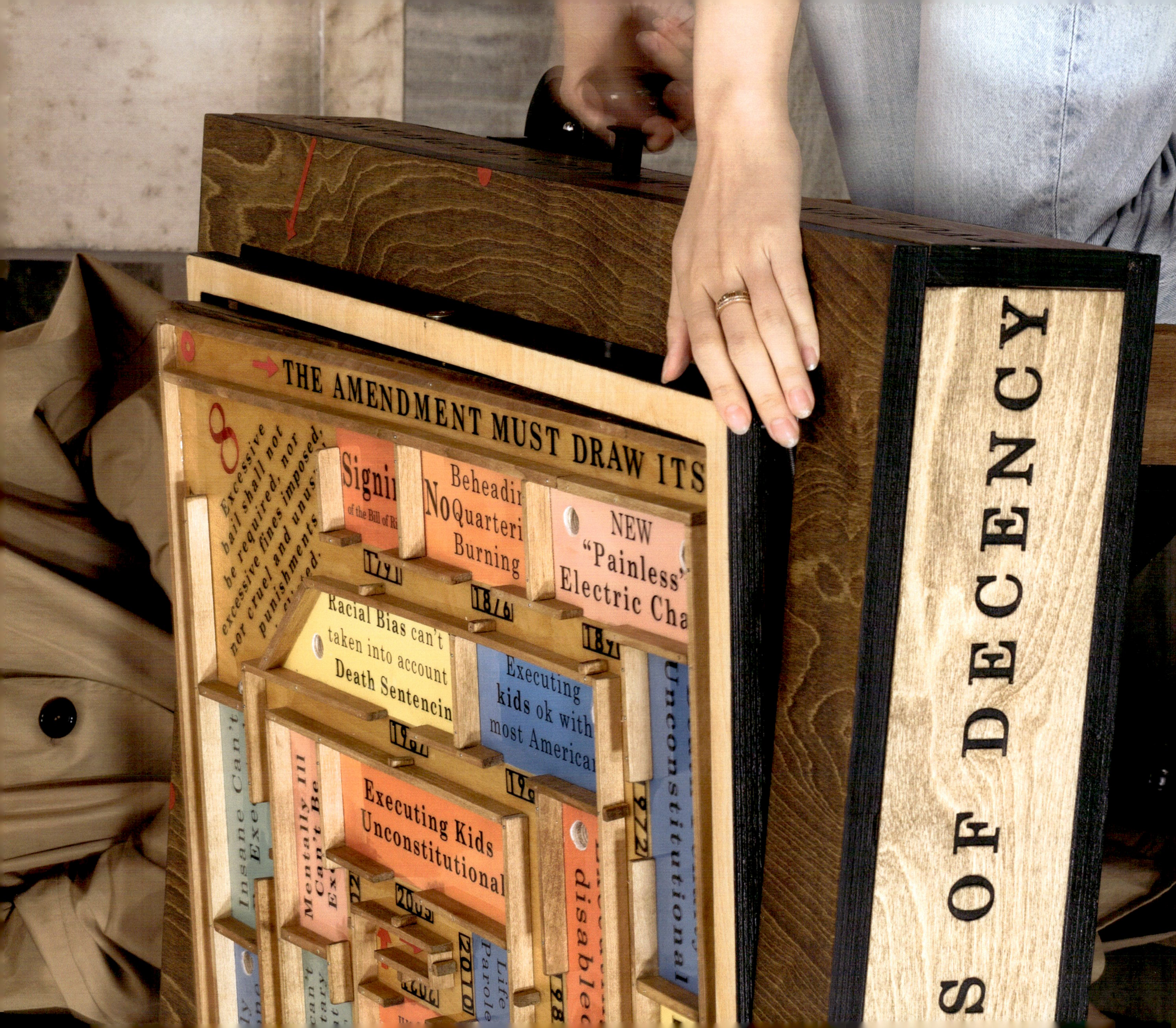
THE AMENDMENT MUST DRAW ITS
Excessive bail shall not be required, nor excessive fines imposed, nor cruel and unusual punishments inflicted.
Signi of the Bill of Ri
Beheadi NoQuarteri Burning
NEW "Painless" Electric Cha
1791
1816
1871
Racial Bias can't taken into account Death Sentencin
Executing kids ok with most American
Unconstitutional
1987
1972
19
Insane Can't Exe
Mentally Ill Can't Be Exe
Executing Kids Unconstitutional
disable
Life Parole
2005
2010
98
S OF DECENCY

Of the amendments, the Eighth is the one the average American most likely assumes is followed, but its application is also the least likely to be scrutinized. It is also one of the amendments in which the unspoken assumptions of for whom the laws apply most acutely manifest. Blurring the picture of the unequal protections from the carceral system is the radicalized social landscape of the US. What of those who find themselves ensnared by the US legal system yet outside the protections of the Eighth Amendment? White Americans are statistically far less likely to be imprisoned than Black and Hispanic Americans and Indigenous people, leading to disproportionate representation within the carceral system. If someone's race sets them apart from the imagined "just" American, is the average American in turn likely to express concern about unjust bails, fines, and punishments?

One of the more useful tools for understanding how games function is systems dynamics, a framework for making sense of how complex machines and social practices operate and impact those who come in contact with them. Simply put by Donella Meadows, one of the most important systems theorists, a system is a set of elements whose interactions lead to a particular outcome or purpose. This is a deceptively simple means to unpack the complexities of the world. Often, analyzing a phenomenon contradicts common beliefs and otherwise sheds light on how little we understand about the given phenomenon.

Viewed as a system, the Eighth Amendment's presumed protections are in fact unequally applied, often along lines of race, gender, and other socioeconomic factors. Danielle Isadora Butler's *Evolving Standards of Decency* presents a playable model for the challenges many Americans confront when navigating the three assurances of the Eighth Amendment. Using a gimbaled maze (more often seen at smaller scales as handheld puzzles), Butler asks the player to keep a ball moving toward the center of the maze while avoiding the holes along the way. Each of the holes represents cases in which one of the Eighth Amendment's three guarantees fell short of protecting an individual. The maze as well addresses those who fall outside protections expected by US citizens yet still find themselves ensnared in the US legal system.

The Eighth Amendment builds upon the guarantees of the Fourth and Fifth Amendments, shielding citizens from unfair prosecution, establishing the structure of a trial, and maintaining the presumption of innocence until proven guilty found in the Sixth Amendment. And yet most accused of crimes are assumed to be guilty and therefore not worthy of the protections afforded by the Eighth. The difficulties of solving a gimbaled maze are not so distant from those of everyone gaining access to the full guarantees of the Eighth Amendment.

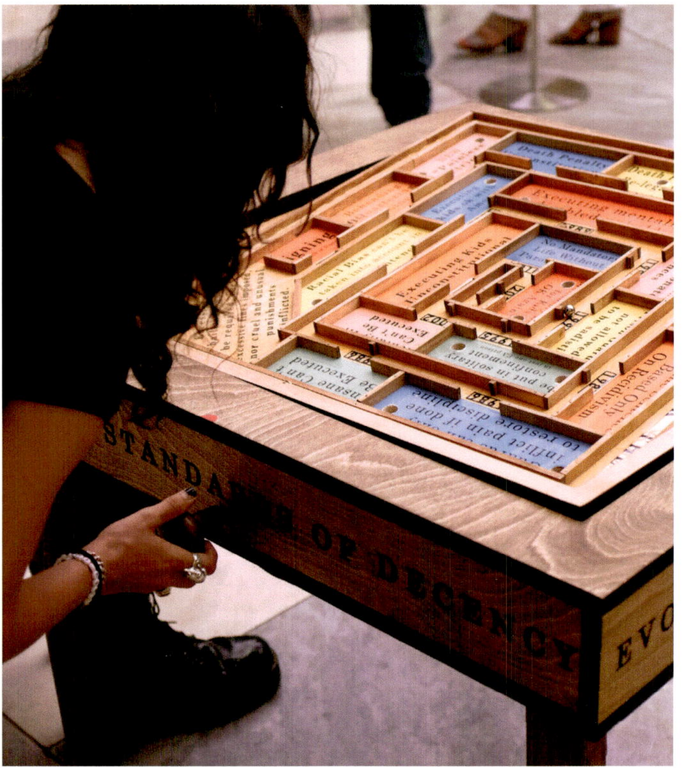

THE NINTH AMENDMENT

The enumeration in the Constitution, of certain rights, shall not be construed to deny or disparage others retained by the people.

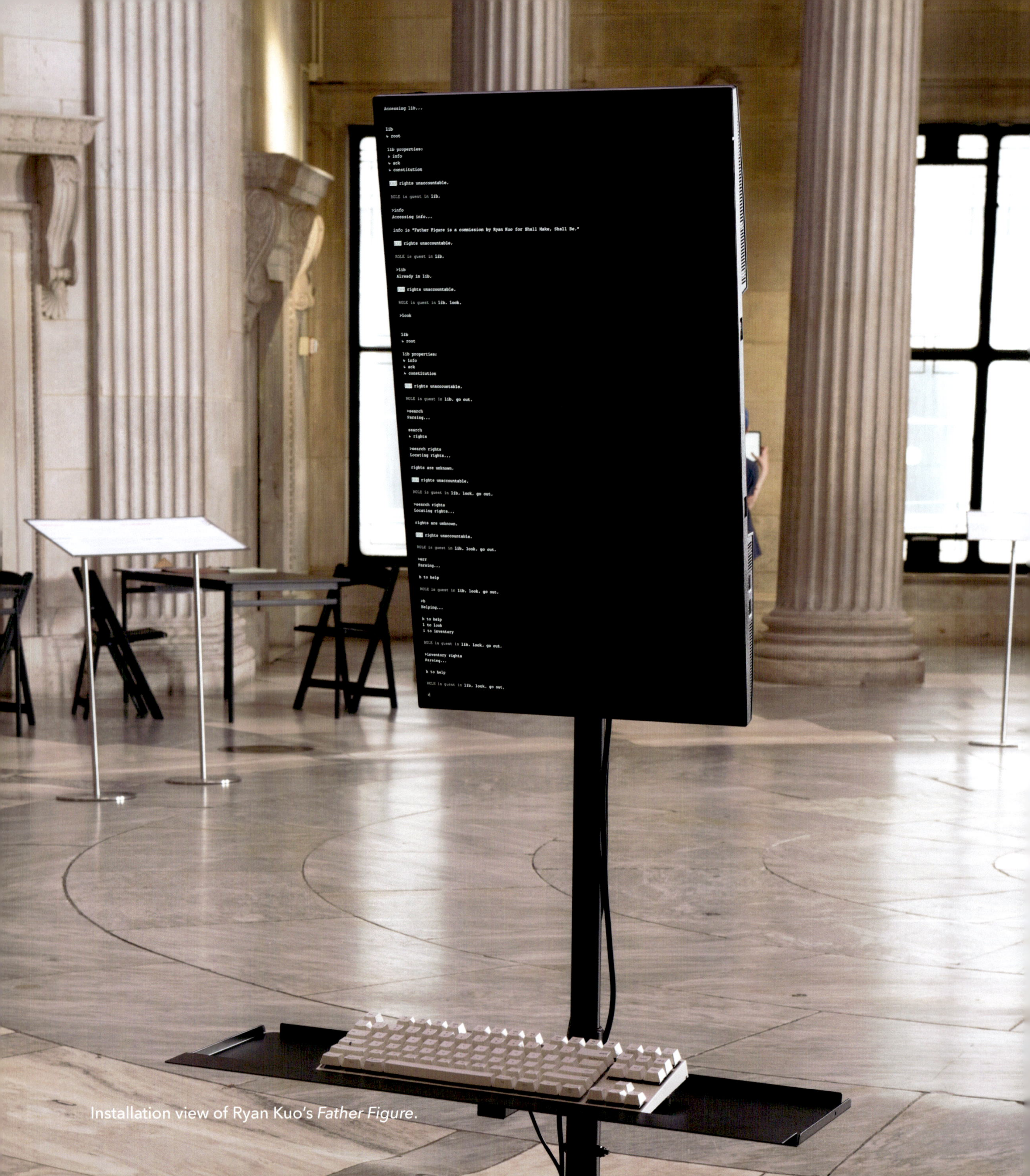

Installation view of Ryan Kuo's *Father Figure*.

Ryan Kuo
Father Figure, 2022
Computer software, keyboard, display stand
Dimensions variable

INTERROGATING THE NINTH AMENDMENT

ERWIN CHEMERINSKY
Dean of the School of Law, University
of California, Berkeley

> The Ninth Amendment . . . is a reminder that the listing of specific rights in the Bill of Rights and the Constitution should not be taken to deny the existence of other liberties.

Although the Ninth Amendment rarely is mentioned in court opinions or in public discussions about the Constitution, it is crucial to understanding many of our most important constitutional rights.

The Constitution, as drafted and approved in 1787, says little about individual rights. One reason for this omission is that its framers were concerned that a listing of rights inevitably would be incomplete. They were afraid that mentioning some liberties would be taken to deny the existence of other rights. But there was substantial opposition to the Constitution in many states because it said so little about individual liberties. Several states narrowly ratified the Constitution and only on the condition that a Bill of Rights would be added.

When the Bill of Rights was drafted, the Ninth Amendment was meant to address this concern. It is a reminder that the listing of specific rights in the Bill of Rights and the Constitution should not be taken to deny the existence of other liberties.

Few Supreme Court cases have mentioned the Ninth Amendment or used it as an explicit basis for decisions. But it is crucial in explaining why it has been permissible for the Supreme Court to protect many important rights, even if they are not mentioned in the text of the Constitution. For example, in 1965, in *Griswold v. Connecticut*, the Supreme Court declared unconstitutional a Connecticut law prohibiting the sale, distribution, or use of contraceptives. The Court concluded that the right to privacy is fundamental and that this includes a right to purchase and use contraceptives.

Justice Goldberg, in a concurring opinion, focused on the Ninth Amendment and how it provides a basis for the Court's protection of this important aspect of autonomy. He explained that rejecting a right to privacy on the ground that it is not mentioned in the Constitution would "violate the Ninth Amendment." He explained that the Ninth Amendment authorizes courts and legislatures to safeguard liberties even if they are not explicitly mentioned in the Constitution or its amendments.

Over time, the Supreme Court has protected many basic rights that are not enumerated in the Constitution's text. For example, under the First Amendment, the Court has deemed freedom of association to be a fundamental right even though it is not among the specific rights delineated. Under the word "liberty" in the due-process clause, the Court has protected a number of crucial freedoms, including the right to marry; the right to procreate; the right to custody of one's children; the right to keep the family together; the right of parents to control the upbringing of their children; the right to purchase and use contraceptives; the right to adult, private, consensual same-sex sexual activities; and the right to refuse medical care.

All of these are basic aspects of liberty, but some question whether it is legitimate for the Supreme Court to protect such rights that are nowhere mentioned in the Constitution or intended by its framers. The Ninth Amendment provides a crucial answer. It means that we should see the Constitution as a statement of our minimum rights. Others, including the courts, can protect more.

Also, Congress and state legislatures, as well as state constitutions and state courts, can protect greater rights than are safeguarded by the United States Constitution.

Congress, for example, has adopted many laws prohibiting race and sex discrimination by private companies, even though such actions would not violate the United States Constitution. Many state courts have interpreted their state constitutions to protect rights that are not protected by the Constitution. For instance, under the United States Constitution there is no right to use privately owned shopping centers for speech purposes. But the California Supreme Court has recognized such a right under the California Constitution. This is permissible because of the Ninth Amendment: states, too, can act to expand rights and have done so on many occasions.

Today, there is a very conservative majority on the Court that is likely to be hostile to the protection of rights that are not enumerated in the Constitution. Their position is that rights like abortion should not be constitutionally safeguarded because they are not explicitly mentioned in the text and were not intended by the Constitution's drafters. But a crucial argument against this view is the Ninth Amendment. It makes clear that it is legitimate to protect rights that are not explicitly mentioned or intended. The Ninth Amendment supports a much more expansive view of rights, and it is the foundation for what the Supreme Court has been doing throughout American history.

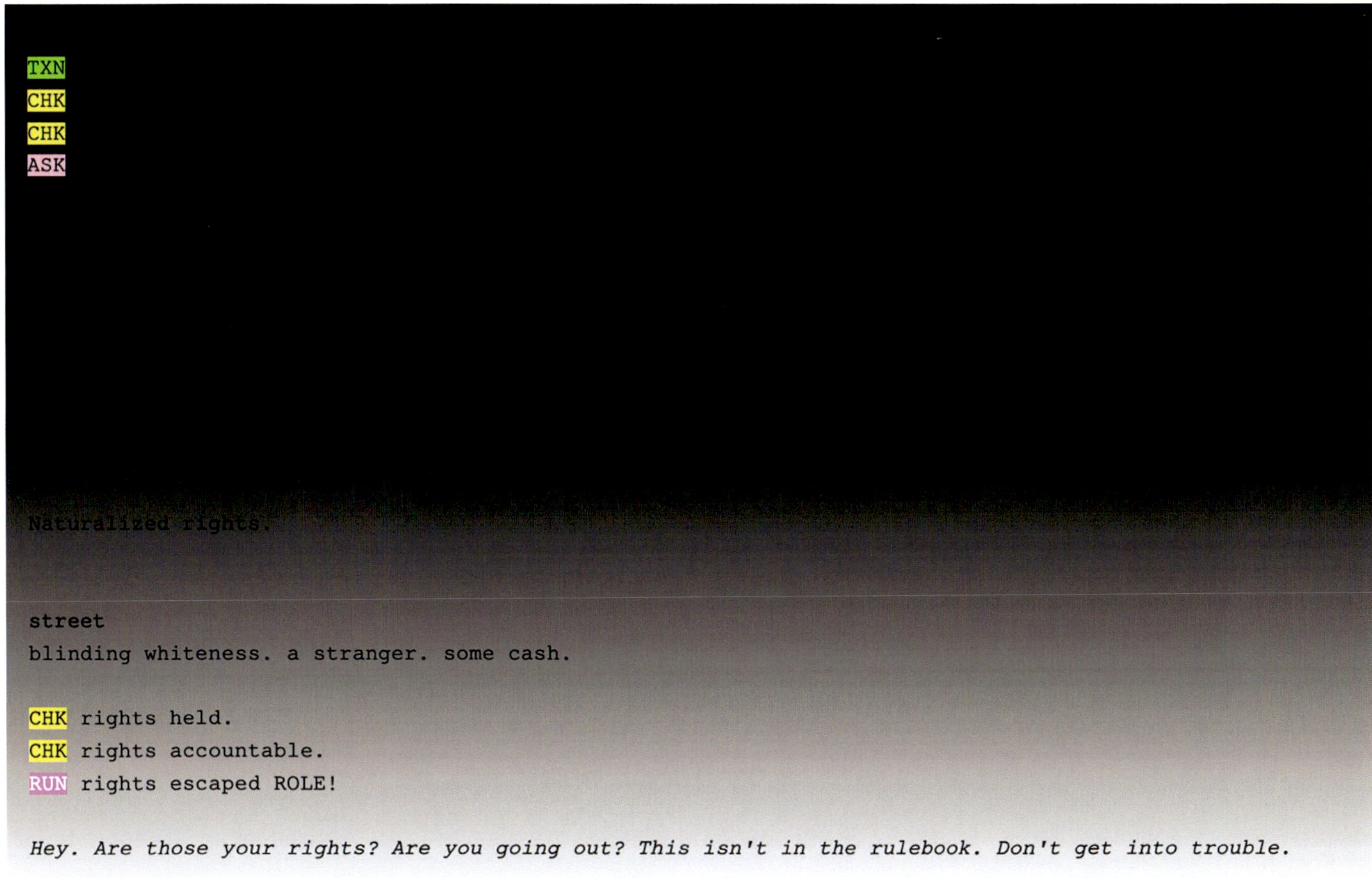

ARTIST COMMENTARY

Ryan Kuo

Father Figure

Father Figure is a text adventure that presents initially as a computer terminal. Using a command-line interface that is intentionally opaque and limiting, one is instructed to locate and reclaim one's missing rights by applying basic text commands. The game begins in earnest when one learns that other commands can be issued to exit the command-line "shell." After exiting the terminal, one finds oneself in a low-fidelity simulation of nature, the space where one's natural rights can be expressed. This leads one eventually to break and enter a House upon pursuing acts of either intentional or accidental violence that echo the US Capitol insurrection of January 6, 2021. What one must confront in the House is the open question of what rights are ultimately "known."

Father Figure considers the Ninth Amendment as a mechanism of whiteness and inserts the user into its scaffold, a text-based simulation of the dynamic at play. In computer usage, the delegation of "rights" does not guarantee freedom but places the user in an inherently compromised position, dependent on the system administrator. This, in turn, prompts a user to grapple directly with how "rights" are defined, granted, and denied—and by whom.

The encounter with the computer aims to impart a material sense of a contradiction at the center of American identity. The Ninth Amendment, which accounts for "certain" rights enumerated as well as "others retained" elsewhere, implies that the rights of the people by nature remain in excess of what can be described. We have a known constitution, but we do not know what constitutes the exception.

This contradiction is inevitably linked to whiteness, the silent majority that holds its tacit rights in reserve like an arms stockpile. It can be argued that the American exception is freedom from accountability, a freedom symbolized and protected by the safety mechanism built into the American contract. For users of the system, then, to what extent is the American dream coterminous with the guarantees of white supremacy? What can define the limit of self-governance?

```
role model properties:
 ↳ bill
 ↳ credit


ERR  rights unaccountable.
CHK  ROLE accountable.
CHK  role model chiding ROLE.
CHK  role model petting rights.


ROLE is guest in home. take rights.


>demand credit
Forcing credit from role model... Failed.


CHK  credit unmoved.
CHK  role model reprimanding ROLE.
CHK  role model feeding rights.
ERR  rights unaccountable.
CHK  ROLE accountable.


ROLE is guest in home. take rights.


>fight dad
Forcing role model... Success!


OOF  role model dazed.
CHK  role model lecturing ROLE.
CHK  role model playing with rights.
ERR  rights unaccountable.
CHK  ROLE accountable.


ROLE is guest in home. take rights.


>|
```

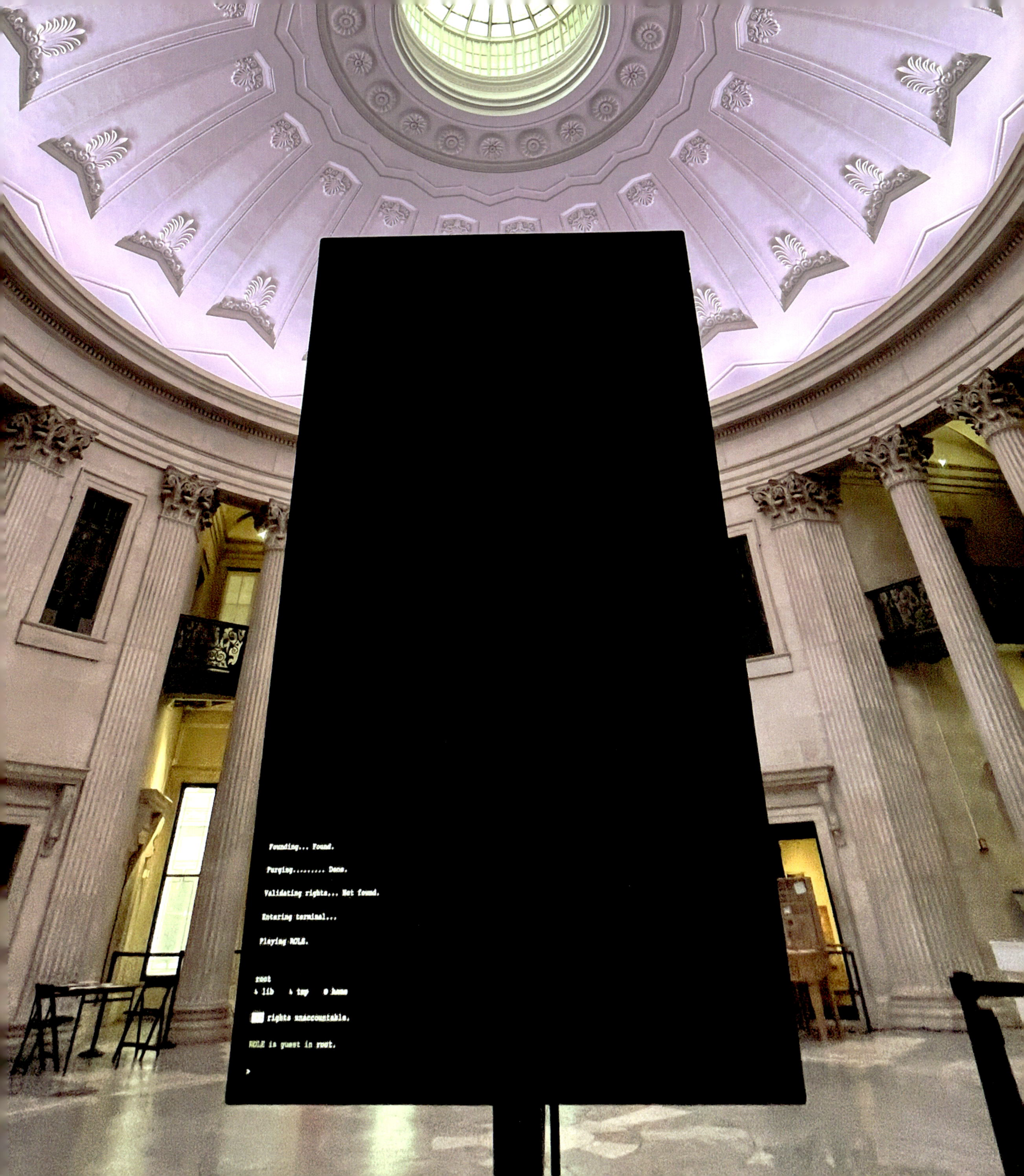

Founding... Found.

Purging.......... Done.

Validating rights... Not found.

Entering terminal...

Playing ROLE.

root
4 lib   4 tmp   0 home

rights unaccountable.

ROLE is guest in root.

>

One way to think about game design is the creation of spaces of possibility inside of which players play. The Ninth Amendment concerns itself with making clear that the space of possibility defined by the Constitution and its amendments will always be incomplete and subject to change. Depending on your perspective, the Ninth Amendment functions as an acknowledgment, a backstop, a tool, or a trap. As an acknowledgment, the Ninth recognizes the limits of its authors' ability to capture in the Constitution all important rights, both those known and those yet to be known. As a backstop, the Ninth served to placate those concerned about the Bill of Rights being interpreted as fully defining individual rights under the Constitution. As a tool, the Ninth affords those with deep knowledge of the Constitution the tools to expand the rights minimally outlined in the original document and its amendments. And as a trap, the Ninth allows those in power to change the rules to benefit or harm. In all four cases, the Bill of Rights is made from and about language, and the ways it and the larger Constitution enumerate if not a ruleset, then a value system for the United States.

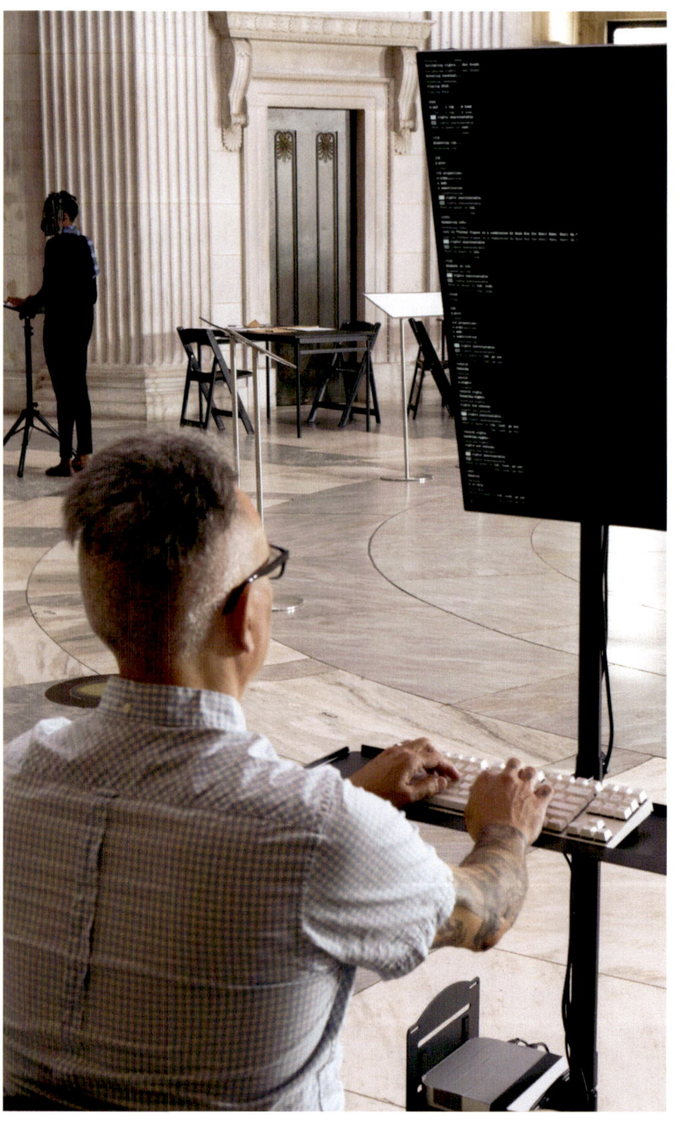

Ryan Kuo's *Father Figure* investigates the Ninth using the text-adventure genre of games within the context of a command-line operating system. Players of text-adventure games interact with a world presented in prose using a very specific dialect to navigate and engage with the story world. For those with fluency in the syntax and vocabulary, engaging the space of possibility authored by the game's creators can be a richly satisfying experience. To someone not versed in the syntax, text adventures (and command-line interfaces) can be frustrating—you quite literally can't do anything if you don't know the right words and phrases to move through and interact with the objects and inhabitants.

Kuo's work is a playable metaphor of the relationship one can have with the space of possibilities for the Constitution as created by the Ninth Amendment. If versed in the logics of text adventures (or US legal theory or a command-line interface), one can move through *Father Figure*; if not familiar with the internal logics, one can at best do nothing, and, more likely, will have the effects of the game (or legal system) happen to them. Kuo asks us to think about who is and who is not allowed to write the new rights, and who does and does not benefit from these new rights.

THE TENTH AMENDMENT

The powers not delegated to the United States by the Constitution, nor prohibited by it to the States, are reserved to the States respectively, or to the people.

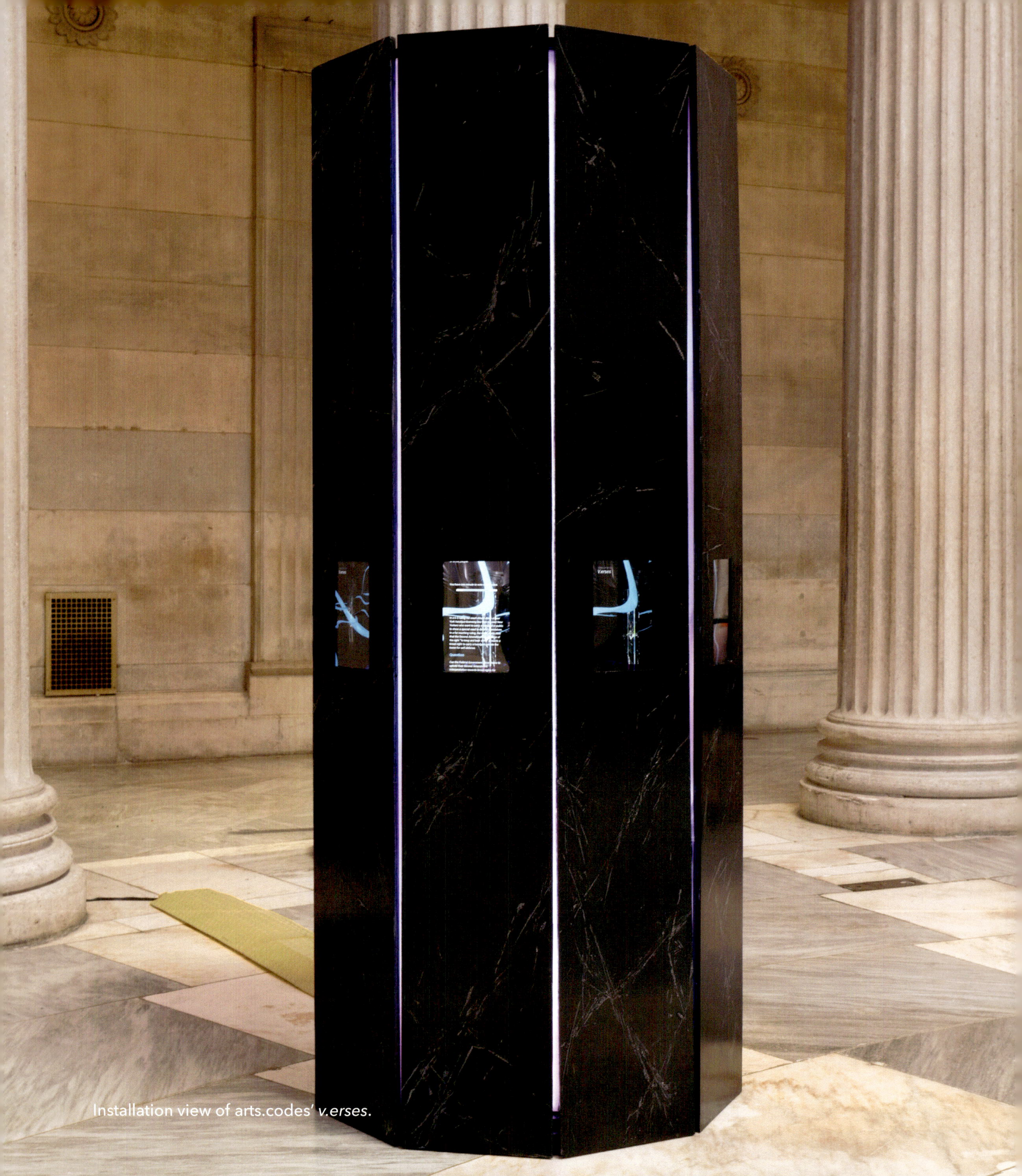

Installation view of arts.codes' *v.erses*.

arts.codes (Melissa F. Clarke and Margaret Schedel)

v.erses, 2022
With engineering assistance by Kari Barry and
Omkar Bhatt, networking by Nick Hwang, music
interaction by Susie Green, and rap lyrics and
performance by Toni Blackman
9-sided wooden column with video screens,
sensors, interactive sound, and LED lighting
Size varies based on location; first iteration
approximately 4 feet by 8 feet

INTERROGATING THE TENTH AMENDMENT

SHARON E. RUSH

Emeritus Professor of Law, University of Florida

> Even the Court struggles to determine where federal power exists and where the federal government unconstitutionally has overstepped the line and entered the space reserved for the states.

The Tenth Amendment symbolizes the concept of "federalism," meaning the people are governed by both the federal and state governments and that there is a boundary line demarcating the areas of power given to the federal government and the powers reserved to the states and the people. This line exists as surely as the equator does, even though both are invisible. Science, of course, has developed a way to measure longitude and latitude so one can tell precisely where the equator is and where one is in relationship to it. While science cannot provide the coordinates to the boundary line between federal and state power, the US Supreme Court—the ultimate voice of the Constitution's meaning—held long ago that the Tenth Amendment is a truism, meaning it speaks for itself as if the boundary between federal power space and states' rights space were as easily discernable as the equator. Yet even the Court struggles to determine where federal power exists and where the federal government unconstitutionally has overstepped the line and entered the space reserved for the states.

For example, Article I of the Constitution gives Congress, consisting of the Senate and House of Representatives, the power to regulate commerce among the several states. Notwithstanding this clear grant of power to the federal government, it is not always clear what is and is not within Congress's commerce-clause power. In the famous "wheat" case, *Wickard v. Filburn,* decided in 1942—only one year after stating that the Tenth Amendment is a truism—a unanimous Court held that Congress had the power to limit the amount of wheat farmers could grow. When a farmer exceeded the limit and grew wheat for his own family-farm consumption, the Court held that, although one farmer exceeding the limit might have a "trivial" effect on interstate commerce, if a lot of farmers were to do the same, the aggregate economic effect of homegrown wheat would substantially affect interstate commerce. Then, in 1995, in a 5–4 decision, the Supreme Court held that Congress's commerce-clause power does not extend to criminalizing the mere possession of guns near schools, reasoning that possession of a gun is not economic or commercial activity. The Court held that to accept the argument that violence in schools substantially affects interstate commerce, especially without specific evidence, would essentially make Congress's commerce-clause power unlimited. Reasonable people might agree or disagree with either or both cases, and the decisions reflect different times in history with different justices interpreting the scope of Congressional power.

Indeed, how to interpret the Constitution is often at the center of conversations about the legitimacy of a decision by the Supreme Court. Realistically, the Court's interpretations of the Constitution necessarily affect the balance of power between the federal and state governments. Complicating any search for a definitive federal-state boundary line is the reality that sometimes the federal and state governments exercise similar powers. For example, both levels of government have taxing power. It is no wonder that the boundary between federal and state power is inexact. This is the nature of federalism.

But it is true that federal power is not unlimited. The Tenth Amendment's language leaves no doubt that the boundary between federal and state power exists. Indeed, just as the equator represents the boundary line between the northern and southern hemispheres—even though a ship could straddle it and be in both hemispheres simultaneously—the federal-state boundary line is exactly what the Tenth Amendment represents.

Accordingly, the shifting of power with respect to the federal-state boundary line can be expected because in a healthy democracy the people understand they will "win sometimes and lose sometimes." Imagine a heart monitor where a beating heart is represented by an ongoing wavelength that steadily rises and falls, rhythmically signaling life. Like this wavelength, sometimes the people's wishes rise to the top in victory, and at other times they sink to the bottom in defeat. Victory or defeat can come regardless of a person's way of participating in the democratic process. The people's wishes can be expressed directly through their votes or indirectly through their elected federal and state representatives. And sometimes judges' decisions, including those of the Supreme Court justices, can sweep a person to the top of the wavelength in agreement and contentment or slide them to the bottom in disagreement and disappointment. Importantly, whether one is riding the top of the wavelength or striving to get back up on top of it, participants in a democracy understand that there are no constant losers because that would signal the death of democracy—a flatline. Indeed, so long as the people have hope that they can make a difference through their constitutional right to participate and be heard, democracy will never flatline.

Thus, notwithstanding the imprecision and fluctuation in demarcating the federal-state boundary line, it exists and is constantly present. In this way, the importance of the Tenth Amendment cannot be overstated. It is the lifeline to understanding what every part of the Constitution means. The Tenth Amendment breathes life into our democracy because federalism—the dynamics between the federal and state governments and how they govern the people and protect their democratic rights—truly is the heart of the Constitution.

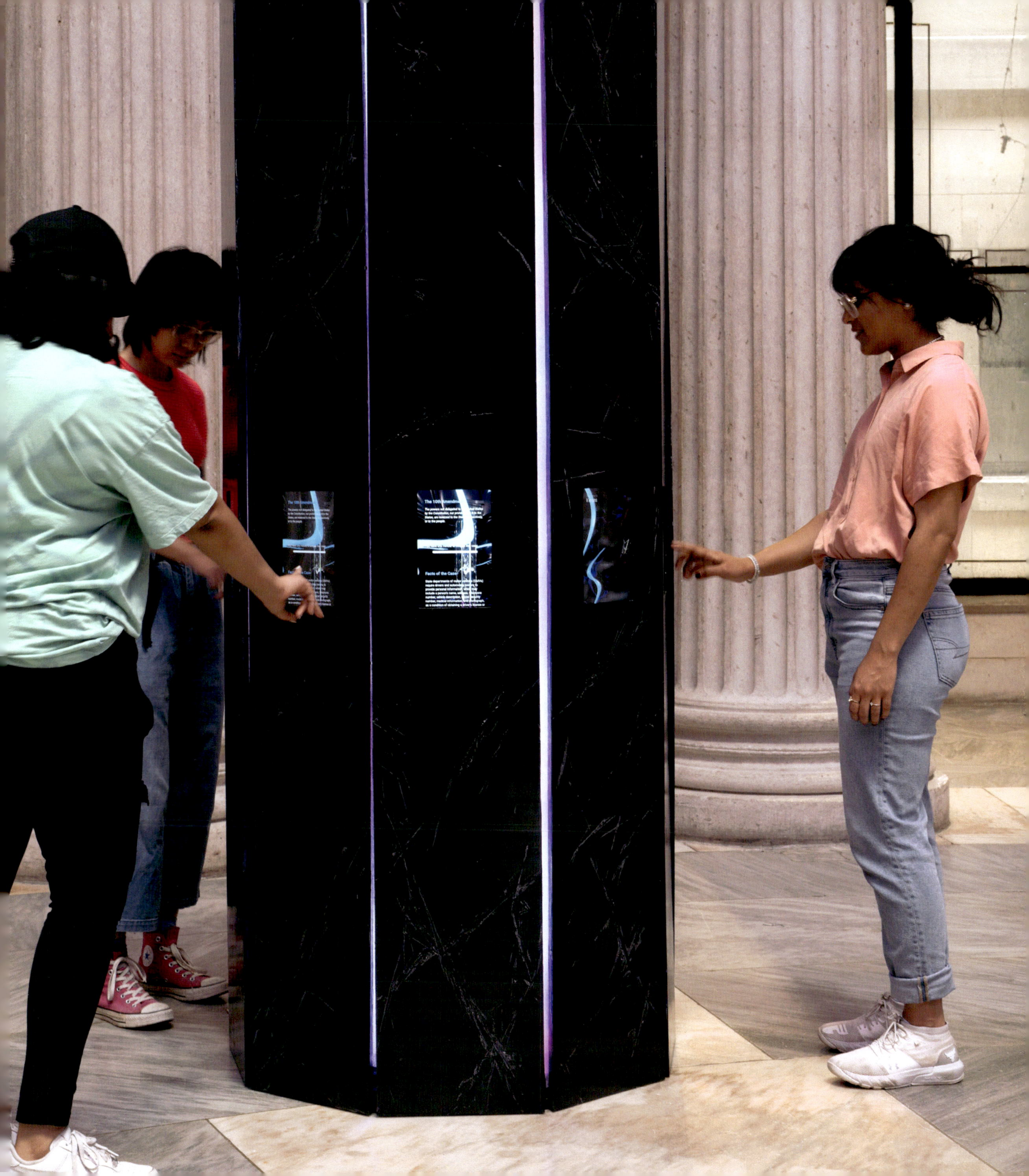
The 10th Amendment
The powers not delegated to the United States by the Constitution, nor prohibited by it to the States, are reserved to the States respectively, or to the people.
Facts of the Case:
State departments of motor vehicles (DMVs) require drivers and automobile owners to provide personal information, which may include a person's name, address, telephone number, vehicle description, social security number, medical information, and photograph, as a condition of obtaining a driver's license or

v.erses is an interactive musical game for multiple players. Players approach a nine-sided column with touchscreens that give a summary of a case and the opportunity to give the power to the Federal Government or the States/People. These results are tallied by a computer and create the rules that the gesturally controlled music then follows. Anyone in the space can play the music by interacting with sensors embedded in the column. If all powers are delegated to the Federal Government, the resulting music becomes a repetitive, uninteresting loop that does not respond at all to the gestural input from the players. Alternatively, if all powers are delegated to the States/People, the music becomes too responsive and chaotic. Players must create a balance between the control of the Federal Government and the freedom of the States/People in order to create an aesthetically pleasing result.

The Tenth Amendment has been called both mysterious and remarkably clear. In one sense it is "but a truism," yet in the 1970s the Supreme Court decided that this truism has teeth. Both Clarke and Schedel were born in this time of transition, where cases decided by judicial interpretations of the Tenth Amendment are becoming more numerous and more partisan. The Supreme Court has relatively recently

Early concept art from arts.codes' proposal for the work. The artists conceived of the piece as modular, with elements added or removed based on the installation context.

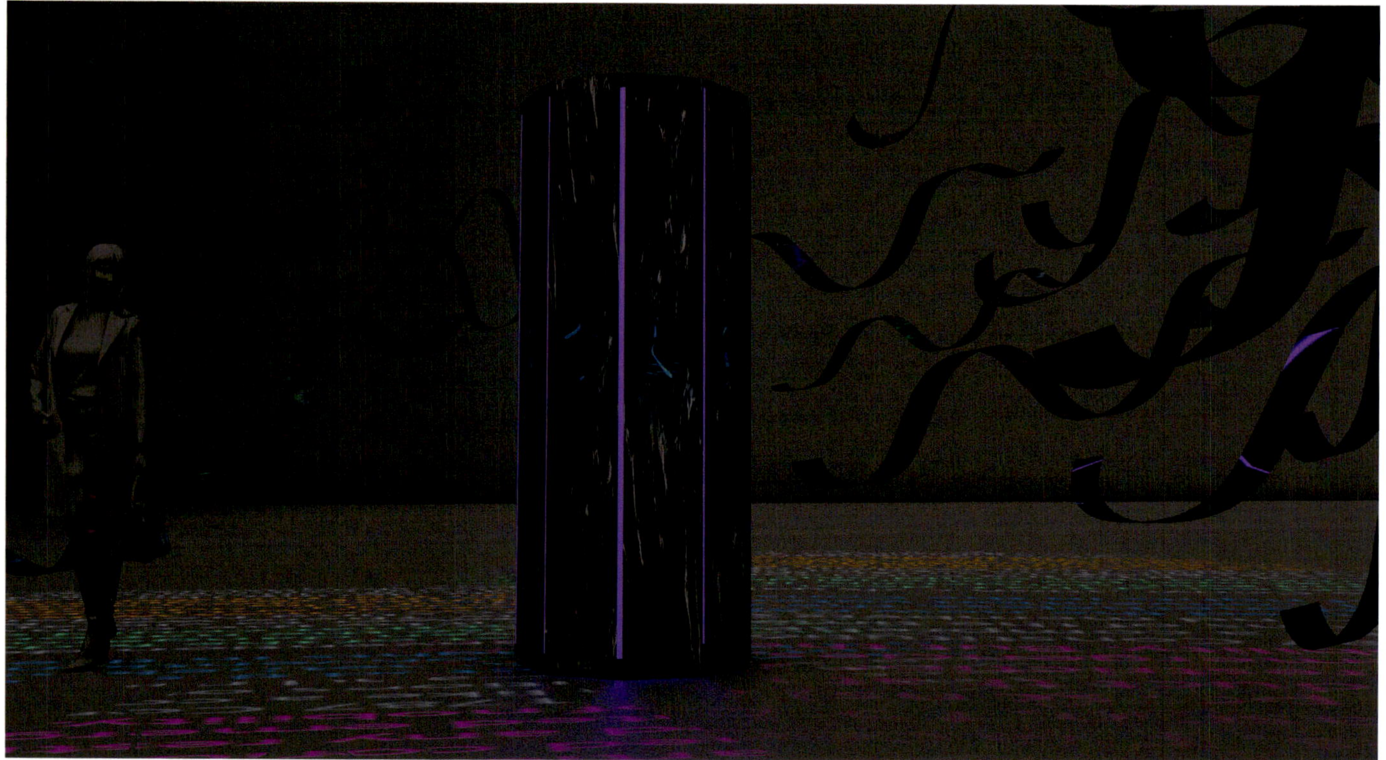

found "judicially-enforceable limits on the power of the federal government to regulate states" in *New York v. United States* (1992), where the Court decided the federal government cannot commandeer state governments into the service of federal regulatory purposes. In 2011, the Court decided that individuals can challenge federal laws on the basis of the Tenth Amendment. It is expected that a challenge to the individual mandate in the Affordable Care Act will also be decided by a nuanced understanding of the limits of federal powers. James Madison wrote, "The powers delegated by the proposed Constitution to the Federal Government are few and defined. Those which are to remain in the State Governments are numerous and indefinite." We drew inspiration for this game from the separation of powers in the Tenth Amendment and from the specialized research area within Human Computer Interface (HCI) called New Interfaces for Musical Expression (NIME). Our system works on a special web-based application called CollabHub, developed by Nick Hwang, which allows us to easily interface inputs such as tablets and sensors with the computer systems running the output of sounds and lights.

The Federal Government Interface (FGI) is a single seven-foot-tall nine-sided wooden column painted to resemble black marble. At the joints between sides of the column there are cracks that let LED lights shine through; each side also has an embedded touchscreen. The screen displays information about previous Court cases involving the Tenth Amendment and allows participants to vote for federal control or state/personal control. The summaries were developed using Oyez, a free multimedia archive devoted to making the Supreme Court of the United States accessible to everyone and created by Cornell's Legal Information Institute (LII); Justia; and the Chicago-Kent College of Law.

When developing the concept for *v.erses*, we were particularly struck by the final clause of the Tenth Amendment, which reads "are reserved to the States respectively, or to the people." This unambiguously reserves all nondelegated power to its original source, the people. The States/People Instrument (SPI) is a site-specific multiplayer sensor that sends information about participants' gestures to the FGI. The decisions made using the FGI control what kind of sonic and visual mappings are possible through players' interaction with the SPI. Essentially the decisions made by the participants on the federal government powers decide the affordances, or what is possible, of the musical game.

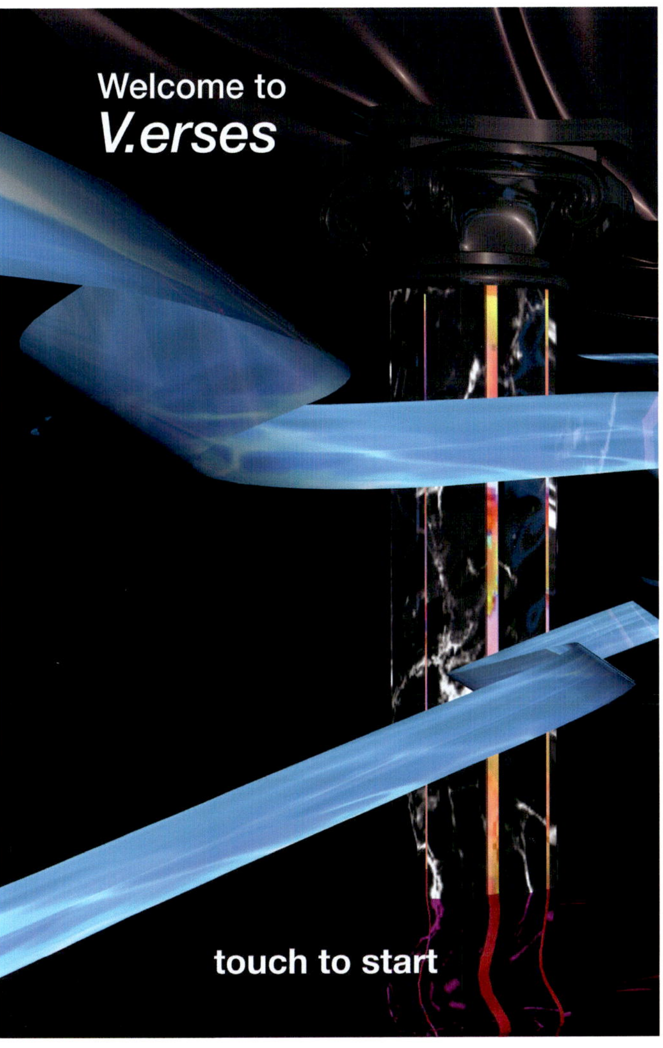

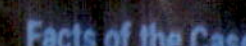

Facts of the Case
State departments of motor vehicles (DMVs) require drivers and automobile owners to provide personal information, which may include a person's name, address, telephone number, vehicle description, Social Security number, medical information, and photograph, as a condition of obtaining a driver's license or registering an automobile. Finding that many States sell this information to individuals and businesses for significant revenues, Congress enacted the Driver's Privacy Protection Act of 1994 (DPPA), which established a regulatory scheme that restricts the States' ability to disclose a driver's personal information without the driver's consent.
Question

The 10th Amendment
The powers not delegated to the United States by the Constitution, nor prohibited by it to the States, are reserved to the States respectively, or to the people.
You have one minute to vote on this case.
Facts of the Case
State departments of motor vehicles (DMVs) require drivers and automobile owners to provide personal information, which may include a person's name, address, telephone number, vehicle description, Social Security number, medical information, and photograph, as a condition of obtaining a driver's license or

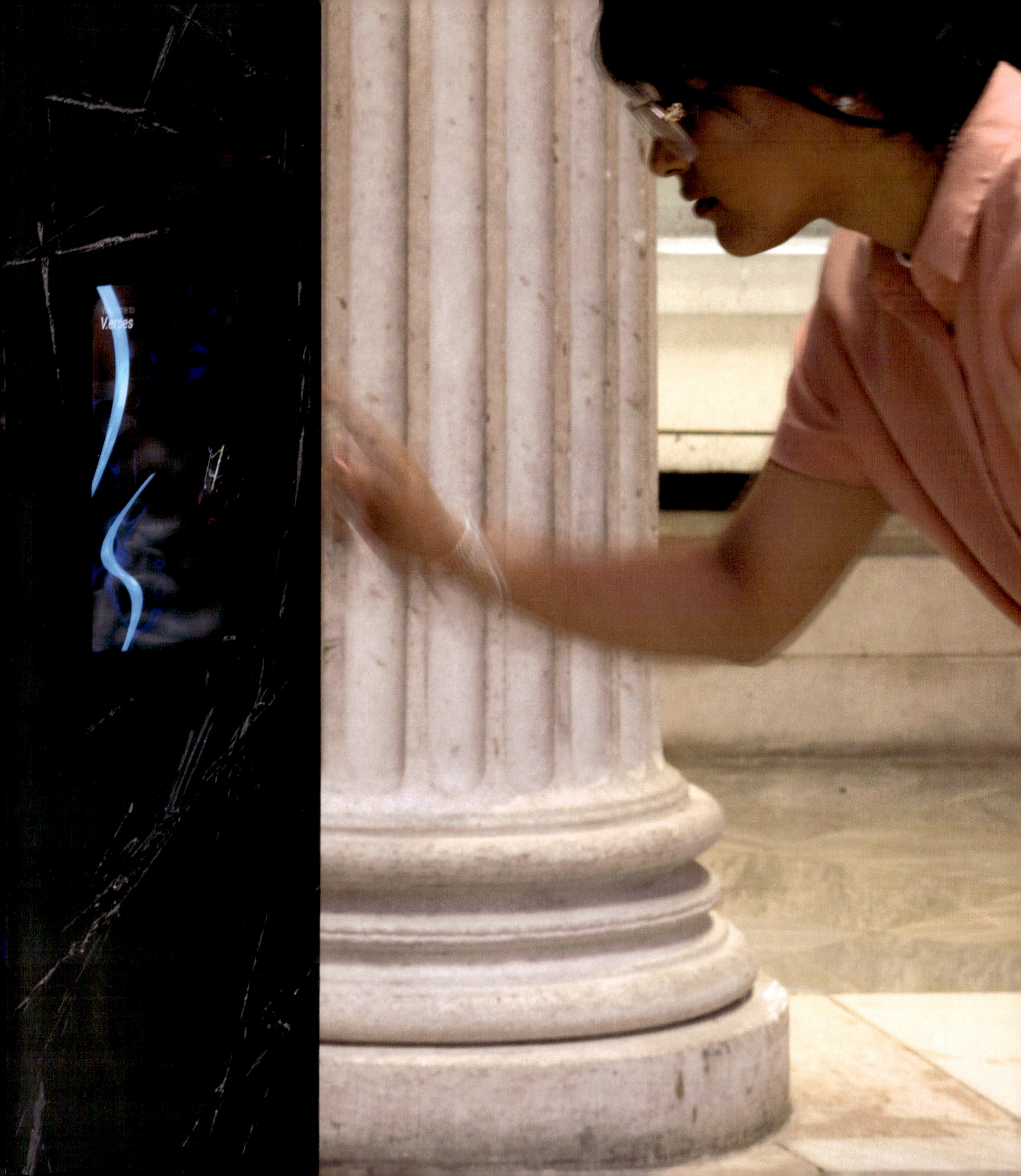
Verses

CURATOR COMMENTARY

Rules are written to be interpreted. How accurate that interpretation will be, and what beauty or lack thereof might be found in that rule's execution, depends on who reads and executes. If read by a computer—software, in other words—the interpretation will likely be strict, assuming the programmer wrote precise instructions. If read by a person, the interpretation will vary, and the way it is executed even more so. With games, there is a notable difference between video games and board games, card games, sports, and other forms of play adjudicated by players. The "wiggle room" of human interpretation and execution is much more variable than that of a computer. With the Constitution—thus far interpreted and run by people—the results are closer to that of a board game, subject to "house rules," regional play patterns, the values and beliefs of the reader, and so on.

The Tenth Amendment is a great example of this. As a rule written for interpretation and execution, it is understood both as a clear and concise declaration of the limitations of federal government reach and also as an open-ended and malleable line marking the boundaries and overlaps of federal and state governance. Beauty is in the eye of the beholder. If one person's idea of a beautiful government is one of minimal federal oversight, then the Tenth Amendment is a precisely phrased instruction. Another person's idea of beautifully conducted governance involves an equitable and expansive oversight of all states and citizens, leading to an interpretation of the Tenth as inclusively speaking to the people, regardless of their state of residence.

arts.codes' *v.erses* explores the inherent tensions and malleability of the Tenth Amendment. Players have two means of engagement with the large musical installation, creating a push and pull between the Federal Government Interface and the States/People Instrument. Actions made on the Federal Government Interface will impact the options available via the States/People Instrument. And the States/People Instrument will in turn impact the sounds produced by the work as a whole. The interplay between the two creates a sonic meditation on the ever-shifting conceptions of the United States of America as a nation of discrete states and as a nation of unified individuals.

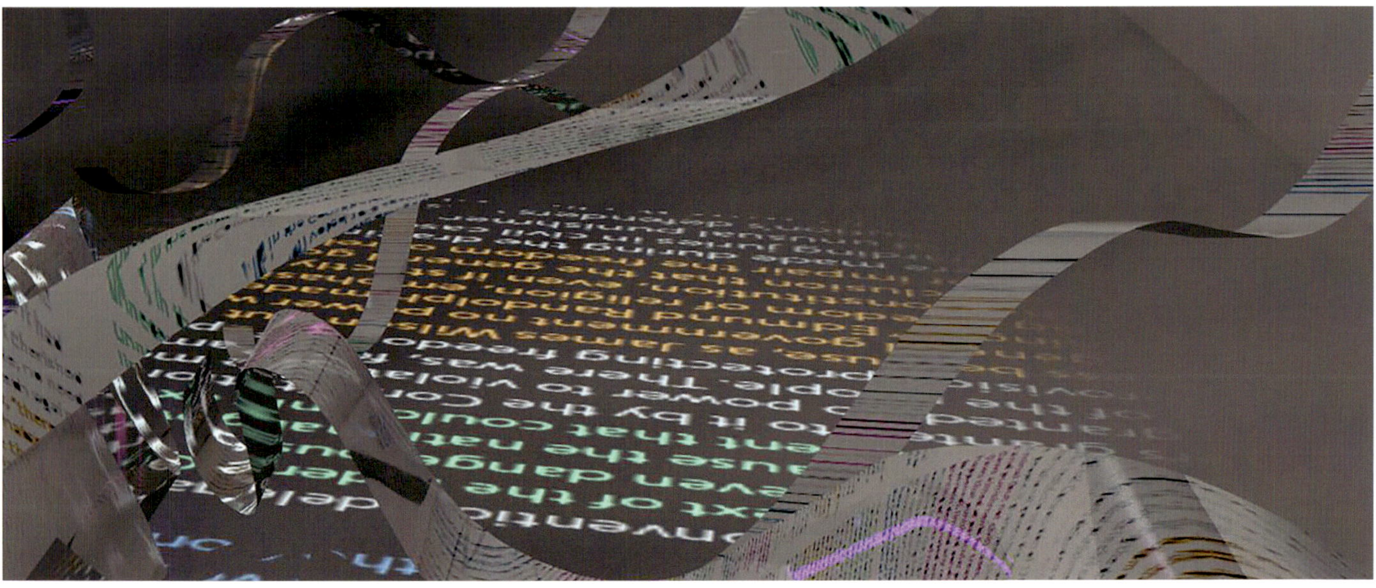

CONTRIBUTOR BIOGRAPHIES

DEBORAH N. ARCHER is the president of the American Civil Liberties Union, a professor of clinical law, and a cofaculty director of the Center on Race, Inequality, and the Law at New York University School of Law. Archer is also a nationally recognized expert on civil liberties, civil rights, and racial justice, as well as an award-winning teacher and legal scholar whose articles have appeared in leading law reviews. Prior to full-time teaching, she worked as an attorney with the American Civil Liberties Union and the NAACP Legal Defense and Educational Fund Inc., where she litigated in the areas of voting rights, employment discrimination, and school desegregation. Archer previously served as chair of the New York City Civilian Complaint Review Board, the nation's oldest and largest police-oversight agency.

ARTS.CODES is an artist collective and open-source distribution platform, codirected by Margaret Schedel and Melissa F. Clarke, that celebrates art with computational underpinnings. **http://arts.codes**

Melissa F. Clarke is a Brooklyn-based educator, designer, and artist working at the intersections of data, science, and design. In her work, she extrapolates interdisciplinary research into multimedia installations, generative environments, audiovisual sculptures, performances, and printed images. A graduate of NYU ITP, Clarke has taught media arts at SUNY Stony Brook and has participated in residencies at Pioneer Works, the Simons Center for Geometry and Physics, and Visible Futures Labs at SVA.

Margaret Schedel transcends the boundaries of disparate fields to produce integrated work at the nexus of computation and the arts. With an interdisciplinary career blending classical training in cello and composition, digital-audio research, and computational-arts education, she is internationally recognized for the creation and performance of ferociously interactive media. Her research in the sonification of gesture and data takes form in interactive opera, VR, and video games. Schedel is a professor and codirector of computer music at SUNY Stony Brook.

MONICA C. BELL is an associate professor of law at Yale Law School and an associate professor of sociology at Yale University. Her areas of expertise include criminal-system policy, policing, welfare law, housing, race and the law, qualitative research methods, and law and sociology.

PETER BRADLEY is a conceptual artist whose recent work is about computers and metaphysics. Applied first to music and the concept of keys, and now to language and the notion of semantic similarity, his practice aims to test the limits of computation, to capture the meaning of an idea as its being is reduced to quantity. He lives in New York City and tours as a member of Japanese Breakfast.

DANIELLE ISADORA BUTLER designs experiences, installations, and objects that create new opportunities for emotional connection. She has designed and produced playgrounds that teach about cooperation, multisensory poetry archives that encourage deep listening, and large-scale games that connect participants to their locales. Her skills in human-centered design extend from a background that combines arts education, creative technology, and restorative justice. Butler believes that building relationships is the key to engaging people in issues that feel too large or abstract to comprehend. She is especially passionate about improving access to water and using creative interventions to deepen New Yorkers' relationship to their harbors. She is a cofounder of both the Tideland Institute and the Awesome Foundation's On the Water organization, which support cultural initiatives on New York waters. https://www.dfunkadelica.com

JENNIFER CARLSON is an associate professor of sociology and government and public policy at the University of Arizona whose work examines gun politics, policing and public law enforcement, the politics of race and gender, and violence. Her first book, on the politics of gun carry, *Citizen-Protectors: The Everyday Politics of Guns in an Age of Decline*, was published in 2015 by Oxford University Press. Her next book project is tentatively titled *Not with a Bang but a Whimper: Guns, Crisis and the Edge of Democracy*, and examines gun-law enforcement in Arizona, California, and Michigan through interviews with police chiefs and observation of gun-licensing procedures.

ARNAB CHAKRAVARTY is a designer, technologist, and educator with a background in building interfaces for communities overlooked by dominant technology platforms. Previously, he worked as an ethnographer and designer in several multinational organizations; at NYU ITP, his interests have focused on living with the things that he makes, creating immersive experiences for co-liberation, and discovering what makes people touch things. His work has been shown at venues including FABLearn, No Quarter, Bengaluru Maker Faire, Kochi Biennale, and NYC Media Lab.

ERWIN CHEMERINSKY is the dean and Jesse H. Choper Distinguished Professor of Law at the University of California, Berkeley, School of Law. He is the author of fourteen books, including leading treatises and casebooks on constitutional law, criminal procedure, and federal jurisdiction. His most recent book, *Presumed Guilty: How the Supreme Court Empowered the Police and Subverted Civil Rights*, was published by Norton in 2021. He also is the author of over two hundred law-review articles and frequent op-ed pieces. He regularly argues appellate cases, including in the United States Supreme Court.

CHERISSE SANTA CRUZ DATU was raised on the island of Guam. A first-generation Filipino American, she was born to Kapampangan parents who, despite not playing games themselves, fostered her love for them—perhaps because her Game Boy kept her quiet during long car rides. She is currently a video producer at Bethesda Softworks. She previously worked in video at ESPN's *The Undefeated* and Al Jazeera's *The Stream*. Datu received her master's degree in game design and her bachelor's degree in film and media arts from American University. A video producer with a background in broadcast-news editing and digital entertainment, she finds comfort in creating small forms of playable art to help process current events.

R. LUKE DUBOIS is a composer, artist, and performer who explores the temporal, verbal, and visual structures of cultural and personal ephemera. An active visual and musical collaborator, DuBois is the coauthor of Jitter, a software suite for the real-time manipulation of media developed by San Francisco–based software company Cycling '74. He appears on nearly twenty-five albums, both individually and as part of the avant-garde electronic group the Freight Elevator Quartet. DuBois has lived for the last twenty-eight years in New York City. He is the codirector of the programs in integrated design and media (IDM) at the NYU Tandon School of Engineering. His artwork is represented by bitforms gallery in New York City. **http://lukedubois.com**

JESSICA M. EAGLIN is a professor of law at Indiana University Maurer School of Law. Her research examines the expansion of technical legal practices in criminal administration as a response to the economic and social pressures of mass incarceration. She is a leading expert on algorithms in criminal sentencing, with recent work exploring the perils this technology presents for historically marginalized groups, the courts, and society more broadly. Prior to law teaching, she worked as counsel at the Brennan Center for Justice at NYU School of Law. She also clerked for the Honorable Damon J. Keith for the Sixth Circuit Court of Appeals. Professor Eaglin graduated from Spelman College. She earned her JD and MA in literature from Duke University.

RYAN KUO creates works that are process based, diagrammatic, and caught in a state of argument. He appropriates video games, productivity software, web design, and text to produce circuitous and unresolved movements that track the passage of objects through white escape routes. He holds a master's degree in art, culture, and technology from MIT and has held residencies at Pioneer Works and the Queens Museum Studio Program. Kuo's works have been shown in venues such as Queens Museum, TRANSFER, and bitforms gallery, and are distributed online at left gallery. His recent and forthcoming projects include *File: A User's Manual*, an artist's book about aspirational workflows modeled after software guides for power users; and *Faith*, a conversational AI agent that zealously embodies the blind "faith" underpinning both white supremacy and miserable white liberalism. Kuo lives and works in New York City. He is not a programmer.

GOLAN LEVIN is a professor of electronic art at Carnegie Mellon University, where he holds courtesy appointments in architecture, computer science, design, and entertainment technology. Since 2009, Levin has also served as director or codirector of CMU's Frank-Ratchye STUDIO for Creative Inquiry, a laboratory for antidisciplinary research across the arts, science, technology, and culture. Levin's work explores new intersections of machine code and visual culture, combining equal measures of the whimsical, the provocative, and the sublime in a wide variety of media. With Tega Brain, he is coauthor of *Code as Creative Medium* (MIT Press, 2021), an educator's guide for teaching computational art and design. **http://flong.com**

ANDY MALONE holds a bachelor's degree in architecture from the University of Detroit Mercy and has worked in the exhibit-design and custom-furniture industry for more than twenty-five years. Notable clients include Google, Twitch, Konami, Salesforce, Dolby, LG, Dodge, HP, T-Mobile, and Bethesda Games. His playable sculptures and games have been shown in more than seventy-five exhibitions since 1995, including two recent solo exhibitions: *Play Room* (2017) and *Happy Accidents* (2019). As a curator of game arts, Malone co-organized *Game Show Detroit* (2006) at the Contemporary Art Institute of Detroit and *Game Show NYC* (2011) at Columbia University. Malone also curated the *BravoBRAVO! Art Exhibition* at the Detroit Opera House in 2004 and 2005. Malone currently serves as vice president of HATCH, an interdisciplinary arts center in Hamtramck, Michigan. **http://www.andymalone.com**

IAN MCNEELY holds an MFA in theater arts from Brown University, where he wrote and produced a series of original rock operas. McNeely was awarded the Oregon Shakespeare Festival's 2009 Rex Rabold Fellowship and delivered the keynote speech at their annual HIV/AIDS fundraiser, the Daedalus Project. He is the founder and artistic director of Broken Ghost Immersives, which produces theatrical events inspired by games.

MOAW! is a video-game developer specializing in pixel art. They work to build creative communities through game development, bridging dialogues between STEM and art, and have worked professionally with many companies to make games and pixel-art advertisements. Outside of commercial work, they design open-source game-development assets and engage in accessible education initiatives such as workshops and events through RVA Game Jams and Tutorial Stage. More recently, they were working as a remote-education consultant for CodeVA. **http://moaw.art**

LAINE NOONEY is an assistant professor of media and information industries in the Department of Media, Culture, and Communication at New York University.

LATOYA PETERSON lives at the intersection of emerging technology and culture. She is currently cofounder and CXO at Glow Up Games, a game studio working on their first title set in the world of HBO's *Insecure*. Previously, she was the deputy editor for digital innovation for ESPN's *The Undefeated*, an editor-at-large at Fusion, and the senior digital producer for *The Stream*, a social media–driven news show on Al Jazeera America. In 2018, she soft launched AI in the Trap, a collaborative art project that explores the future of artificial intelligence and predictive policing through a hip-hop lens. In 2016, she produced a critically acclaimed YouTube series on girl gamers that was highlighted on Spotify. She is currently on the advisory board of the Data & Society Institute and the board of visitors for the John S. Knight Journalism Fellowships. She is a US-Japan Leadership Program fellow and a USC Civic Media senior fellow. She is also part of the selection committee for the Museum of Play's World Video Game Hall of Fame.

SHAWN PIERRE is a visiting assistant arts professor at the NYU Game Center and a game designer working to combine new forms of play with different types of media. His work includes voice-controlled adventure games, social deduction SMS games, and physical games where players capture others in nets. In the past, Shawn has created and worked on crowd-based interactive activities, including installments at Graceland, as well as games for major sporting events. As a member and project director of Philly Game Mechanics, Shawn works to build a community where local creators meet new people and share their creative work.

KERAMET REITER is a professor of criminology, law, and society at the University of California, Irvine. She studies prisons, prisoners' rights, and the impact of prison and punishment policy on individuals, communities, and legal systems. She is the author of two books: *23/7: Pelican Bay Prison and the Rise of Long-Term Solitary Confinement* (Yale University Press, 2016) and *Mass Incarceration* (Oxford University Press, 2017). She is the director of LIFTED, a program to offer University of California BA degrees to incarcerated students, and the cofounder of UCI PrisonPandemic, a digital archive of incarcerated Californians' stories of living through the COVID-19 pandemic.

SHARON E. RUSH is the Raymond and Miriam Ehrlich Eminent Scholar and professor emeritus at the University of Florida Levin College of Law. During her thirty-four years on the faculty, she enjoyed countless wonderful hours of intellectual exchanges with bright, insightful, kind, and caring students. Her teaching and research focused on constitutional issues, particularly in the areas of federalism, equality, and race relations. She received her BA and JD cum laude from Cornell University.

MICHAEL E. SHAMMAS is a Forrester Fellow at the Tulane University Law School, where he conducts research and teaches legal research and writing to first-year law students. After graduating from Harvard Law School in 2016, he practiced as a litigator in Manhattan for two years before leaving to work in the federal judiciary and, afterward, in academia. **https://medium.com/@mshammas**; Twitter: **@michaelshammas9**

JOHN SHARP is a professor of games and learning at Parsons School of Design at the New School. He is a member of the game-design collective Local No. 12, the creators of the *Metagame* and *Dear Reader*. John is the author of *Works of Game: On the Aesthetics of Game and Art*, and coauthor of *Games, Design and Play: A Detailed Approach to Iterative Game Design* with Colleen Macklin; *Fun, Taste, and Games: An Aesthetics for the Idle, Unproductive, and Otherwise Playful* with David Thomas; and *Iterate: Ten Lessons in Design and Failure* with Colleen Macklin. John has curated a number of games exhibitions, including at the Museum of the Moving Image and Museum of Design Atlanta. **http://www.heyimjohn.com**

NABIHA SYED is the president of the Markup, an investigative journalism startup that explores how powerful actors use technology to reshape society. Previously, she was vice president and associate general counsel at BuzzFeed. As the company's first newsroom lawyer, she oversaw litigation, including the "Steele Dossier" litigation, as well as select intellectual property, security, international, and cross-company strategic initiatives. Syed has been described as "one of the best emerging free speech lawyers" by *Forbes* magazine. Before BuzzFeed, Syed was an associate at Levine Sullivan Koch & Schulz, a leading media law firm, and the First Amendment fellow at the *New York Times*.

SUJA A. THOMAS is the Peer and Sarah Pedersen Professor of Law at the University of Illinois College of Law. She wrote *The Missing American Jury: Restoring the Fundamental Constitutional Role of the Criminal, Civil, and Grand Juries* (Cambridge University Press) and coauthored *Unequal: How America's Courts Undermine Discrimination Law* (Oxford University Press). She has appeared on CNN speaking about juries, and her work has been featured in the *New York Times*, the *Wall Street Journal*, and *Slate*. Thomas is making a mainstream social-justice documentary film and was a fellow with Kartemquin Films. She graduated from Northwestern University and NYU Law School and practiced law in New York City at the law firms of Cravath, Weil, and Vladeck.

VI TRINH works in digital and traditional media to examine the relationship between ecological and social patterns. A Vietnamese American artist based in Washington, DC, Trinh graduated from the University of Richmond in 2019 with a BA in visual and media arts practice and leadership. She is currently an MFA candidate at Goldsmiths, University of London. Much of Trinh's work is based in and on the internet. Through her interactive digital art, Trinh explores dynamics of power and control, freedom and restraint, and how they manifest in networked media. Themes in Trinh's work include aesthetics in ecological emergency; new temporal realities created by very large-scale phenomena; and the contradiction between the internet as a seemingly free and democratic space and the reality of the internet as a site of exclusionary design, extractive corporatization, technologized colonialism, and the perpetuation of white supremacy. **https://vtrinh.net**

LEXA WALSH makes projects, exhibitions, publications, and objects, employing social engagement, institutional critique, radical hospitality, and community building. Her upbringing as the youngest child of fifteen informs her work, as does practicing collectivity while coming of age in the post-punk scene of the 1990's Bay Area. Embedded in her practice, she works as an arts laborer, organizer, curator, and archivist. Walsh has founded or cofounded several arts platforms, including the Heinz Afterworld Lounge, an experimental music venue; Toychestra, an all-women, all-toy instrument ensemble; Oakland Stock, a branch of the Sunday Soup crowdfunding network; and most recently, the Bay Area Contemporary Art Archive, a platform for the preservation of arts ephemera. Walsh has also worked as an artist-in-residence and/or curator at a variety of arts institutions, including a term as a social-practice artist-in-residence at the Portland Art Museum and several years as a curator and administrator at CESTA, a Czech art center. She holds an MFA from Portland State University's art and social-practice program and a BFA from California College of Arts and Crafts (now California College of the Arts). **https://www.lexawalsh.com**

ALEXANDER ZHANG is a JD-PhD student at Yale who specializes in American legal history. His research focuses on the processes of creating and interpreting legislation, the historical evolution of race, and the relationship between rights and obligations in creating inequality. Zhang received a four-year BA-MA in American studies magna cum laude with exceptional distinction in 2018 from Yale, where he was awarded the university-wide John Addison Porter Prize for outstanding thesis or dissertation in any field.